post scripts

from the Saturday Evening **POST**

POST SCRIPTS

chosen by **JOHN BAILEY**

illustrated by Henry Syverson

MACRAE SMITH COMPANY: PHILADELPHIA: 1952

to Nancy and Dottie

FOREWORD

Americans are fond of telling funny stories. Most of us, however, don't tell them very well. We are apt to begin by saying,
"This is the funniest story I ever heard in my life." This creates
the natural suspicion that the story can't be very good.

We then urge the hearer to stop us if he has heard it before;
and without giving him the slightest chance to do so we proceed
with a garbled version of the story, with much prodding of our
forefinger into his stomach, and with several flashbacks in order
to straighten up significant points—such as, "Oh. I should have
told you that the fellow who is driving the car is a lapidarist and
it's his uncle who smokes cigars, not his sister."—and with so
much helpless laughter and gasping on our own part that the
whole thing becomes unintelligible anyway.

This is apt not to matter much, for it is not uncommon for us
to near the end of the story and discover that we have forgotten
the point. This entails removing our hat to scratch our head, and
for the next five minutes to wonder aloud how that story ended.

I will not, therefore, begin by saying that these are the funniest
stories I ever heard in my life. (Though they are.) I will content
myself by saying simply that I have laughed helplessly at each one.

Visitors to the fifth floor of the Curtis Publishing Company
have been known to turn pale and clutch the nearest executive in
alarm at the hollow cackling proceeding from behind the door
marked Post Scripts.

Within, perhaps I was laughing at the beloved nonsense of
Colonel Stoopnagle, as he speculated on the unusual roundness of
circles; or perhaps I was laughing at Fontaine's perfectly reasonable explanation of why it takes three hours to play Chopin's
Minute Waltz properly.

Both are here for you to read; so is the lilting, rollicking com-
edy of Jacobson; the close-lipped, cynical irony of Stinnett; the
masterfully turned verses of Armour and Jaffray; farce at its very

best, by Ashbaugh; the learned absurdities of Ellis and Crabtree; the darting wit of Nash; the sly, rich humor of Cuppy; the keen eye and the expert rhyming of McGinley; and the delightful rhymes and writings of a new master, C. P. Donnel, Jr.

There is much more, all of it of high quality, by both well-known and comparatively unknown writers. These are our brightest humorists. In each generation there is a handful of writers who have the ability to make us laugh. And if the present crop compares favorably with previous crops it is in no small degree due to the continued existence of the Post Scripts Page.

Almost alone, now, it encourages writers to put on cap and bells and to amuse us for a half hour, when we are tired of putting our shoulder to the wheel, and of thinking serious thoughts.

If the book has a flaw, it is that there are not enough pieces by me. I had wanted to include much more of my own work, but the publisher was of the opinion that to add anything else would ruin the balance of the book, which was already slightly ruined by the fact that there were six pieces too many in the book. He didn't say which six.

—J. B.

post scripts

JUST LEAVE A NOTE, HONEY

WHENEVER I come in at night to be greeted by a pear-shaped silence, I know that somewhere around the house there will be a note. These little documents are remarkable for their brevity and whimsey.

One beauty I've picked at random reads: I'M AT MOTHER'S. WATCH FOR EGG MAN. FEED DOG. WHEN EGG MAN COMES PUT HIM IN THE BASEMENT. HEARD FUNNY NOISE IN CHIMNEY TO-DAY. DO YOU SUPPOSE A BIRD IS IN THERE? BAKED BEANS IN THE OVEN.

It was obvious from this communiqué that I was in for a ticklish evening. A bird in the chimney, baked beans in the oven and either the egg man or the dog, or both, locked in the basement and snarling at each other. As I remember, I put the dog in the attic, locked the egg man in the garage, put my hair up in curlers and went to bed with a good book.

One item of last summer that was worked into a tea towel with colored thread said: IF YOU GET HOME EARLY, WE'VE GONE

Swimming. If You Get Home Late, We'll Be Back by Then and I'll Have Dinner Ready. I spent several days trying to forget that one.

Sometimes the notes will come in series. They start at the front door and cancel each other out as they go through the house. One set that I've had mounted read like this: Gone to Club. Man Called About Noon. Very Urgent. He Was Breathing Hard, But Wouldn't Leave Number. Do You Owe Someone Money? This little jewel was on the hall table just inside the door. A second note lying on the desk in the living room said: May Not Go to Club Today. Breathing Man Called Again at Two. Think Baby Swallowed One of My Earrings.

Prowling on through the house in a slight daze, I came into the kitchen. My wife was standing at the sink, peeling onions.

"Hello," she said. "It wasn't an earring after all. It was a button. I called the doctor and he said not to worry."

"That's nice," I said. "What about the breathing man?"

"Oh, him," she said. "Didn't you read my note? It's on the telephone stand."

I went back in and read the note.

This one said: Forget About Breathing Man. He Had You Mixed up With Someone Who Wanted to Rent a House. Decided not to Go to the Club Today.

With measured tread I walked back through the kitchen.

"Don't go away," said my wife. "Dinner will be ready in a few minutes."

"I'll be out in the back yard," I said.

"Okay," she answered. "I'll call you when we're ready."

"Send me a note," I said.

—DICK ASHBAUGH.

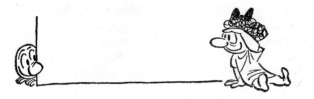

GRIM PARTY

I'M mightily fond of a party.
  When summoned to sup or to dine
Or join in some merriment hearty,
  I practically never decline.
But something incessantly galls me
  When off to the revels I've sped.
It isn't the party appalls me,
  But the hostess with schemes in her head—
The hostess, the terrible hostess,
  Convivial schemes in her head.

Her eye, it is piercing and haggard,
  Her voice has authority's tone.
She cannot let laughter be laggard
  Or well enough ever alone.
It's hey for the pencils and papers
  When drained is the demitasse cup!
She's scheduled some comical capers
  For stirring our intellects up.

No time, now, to pamper digestions
  Or finish a conquest we've made.
We've got to play Answers and Questions
  Or act out some clever charade.

Or maybe she's taken a notion
  With music to harrow the meek,
So someone sings Trees with emotion
  And someone plays Haydn-go-seek.

Perhaps she has made a collection
  Of porcelain pigs of the past,
And we must go round on inspection
  Till adjectives fail us at last.
Or else she must brightly invoke us
  To stare through a dubious dark
At movies—a bit out of focus—
  She took in Yosemite Park.

Oh, nobody's fonder than I am
  Of parties and social requests,
But would that they'd banish to Siam
  The hostess who bullies her guests.
The grim, the implacable hostess
  With grim little plans for her guests.

—PHYLLIS MCGINLEY.

HANDS OFF

DON'T tickle me to find out whether
I'm ticklish. While I'm all together
And uncontorted, fairly seemly,
I'll tell you: yes, I am, extremely.

—RICHARD ARMOUR.

WARM-UP

"WHAT a heavenly day! Aren't you glad that I came?"
"You bet."

"Don't you think that more wives ought to take up the game?"
"Ah . . . sure."

"Would you mind if next time we bring mother out too?"
"Huh?"

"Mercy sakes! Why is everyone starting to boo?"
"Umpires."

"Do they mean those poor men in the funny blue suits?"
"Yeah."

"But that fat man just called them, 'You cross-eyed galoots'?"
"Umpires!"

"What's that sign way out there, like a big crossword puzzle?"
"Scoreboard."

"That galoot down in front—is he wearing a muzzle?"
"Mask!"

"Oh, wouldn't you think they'd be scared of this mob?"
"Uh-uh."

"What on earth do they do for a regular job?"
"Umpire."

"You mean the poor things don't have regular work?"
"Uh-huh."

"Not even part time, like a helper or clerk?"
"Uh-huh."

"This sun's rather hot. Can't we move to the shade?"
"Uh-uh."

"Then, please, will you fetch me some fresh-fruit orangeade?"
"Huh?"

"Never mind. Pretty soon, can't we sit in the bar?"
"Huh?"

"George, don't tell me you're lighting that evil cigar?"
"Uh-huh."

"Just for me, won't you stick to a nice cigarette?"

"Uh-uh."

"I'm a weensy bit tired. Is the game over yet?"

"Uh-uh."

"Have we got to stay on in this heat and this smell?"

"Uh-huh."

"Tell me, what did that man in the muzzle just yell?"

"PLAY BALL!"

—C. P. DONNEL, JR.

LITTLE TALKS ON SCIENCE
How Does a Bicycle Pump Work?

ONE of the hard things for man to understand is the bicycle pump. There doesn't seem to be any sense to it. Yet the bicycle pump is one of the most remarkable inventions in history.

It is all the more remarkable when we consider how little the inventor had to go on. The bicycle had not yet been invented.

One evening in 1864 a boy was sitting in his mother's kitchen watching a teakettle.

Why is it, he asked himself, *that the steam that comes out of the spout doesn't go back in again?*

That boy was Lester W. Pump, father of the modern bicycle pump.

He began to experiment with different lengths of pipe. Some of them, he noticed, were longer than others. These he discarded. Before long he had a crude bicycle pump as we know it today, except that it didn't have any handle. The handle came later, after people found out that without any handle there was no place to grab hold of it. Neither did it have that long rubber thing on the end, that was to prove so important.

The bicycle pump was not an immediate success. People laughed. They said that there was nothing that a bicycle pump could do that a horse couldn't do better. A contest was arranged between a bicycle pump and a horse. When the horse won, Lester was not discouraged. He went back to his shop and set to work. Then, in 1889, there was another contest. The horse won again.

In the crowd was a poor French lad, Armand Velocipede. Seeing the pump gave him an idea. *Why not,* he thought, *a bicycle?* He started work. One year later he was ready. Except that it had no wheels, his bicycle was very similar to the bicycle we are familiar with.

A contest was arranged between the bicycle and a horse. The

horse won. Armand, however, was not discouraged. He went back to his shop.

But the development of the bicycle is another story. It is enough, for the time being, that we have learned how the bicycle pump works.

—JOHN BAILEY.

HOW I MISSED THE FLU

PEOPLE are still talking about their experiences in last winter's flu epidemic and are looking forward eagerly to the next one. I feel left out of every conversation, because I have nothing to talk about. I didn't get the flu.

When it hit our office, Mrs. McCormick, the cashier, told me, "If you're wise, you'll do what my family did in 1918. Put some bear grease up your nose and sip a few teaspoons of Irish whisky morning and night and let it roll around your tongue. It's wonderful protection."

"Then you didn't get the flu in 1918?"

"Well, yes, I did, toward the end of it. But I didn't mind it so much. It wasn't bad at all."

I didn't take this treatment, because when I went to ask Mrs. McCormick the next day whether Scotch whisky would do as well, she was gone. She was home with the flu, and having, I imagine, a hilarious time with it. She didn't come back for three weeks, and I don't blame her.

Miss Gladwyn, who was hired temporarily to fill her place, told me I should get some of the large white tablets she was taking three times a day. "They're a prescription of old Doctor Thompson," she said. "He gave it to me only a month before he died. I don't know what they are, but they're the only thing in the world that does any good. Do you know whose word I have for that?"

I said I couldn't offer a guess; I presumed it was Sir William Osler.

"Billy Doherty, the druggist, told me so himself. He said very few people know about the tablets."

She paused to let the effect sink in, and I looked properly impressed. Naturally the druggists, who make up the prescriptions, are in the best possible position to know which medicines the doctors prescribe only rarely, so as not to give away trade secrets or let people get better too fast.

Miss Gladwyn promised to bring the prescription next morning. Unfortunately, she didn't come back; she took the flu, and before she got better, Mrs. McCormick had returned to work, a little wobbly on her legs and smelling rancid, but in high good spirits.

So, unable to take advantage of anybody's treatment in time, I missed the flu completely. I was forced to go through the entire epidemic season without even a sniffle to talk about.

—STUART TRUEMAN.

COLLEGE TRAINED

WHEN I began on my A.B.,
I thought none knew as much as me;
Now, having passed that milestone by,
I think none knows as much as I.

—R. A. CRABTREE.

SUMMER IS ICUMEN IN

A PRELIMINARY survey conducted by my staff of experts indicates that we are in for a truly memorable summer this year. The United States has a greater backlog of old jelly and pickle glasses than at any other time in its history, so that tenants of beach cottages will be well supplied with drinking glasses. The tin knife-and-fork supply is also adequate, and the consensus is that the 1908 mattress is one of the most durable articles ever produced and can be made to last at least another season by reinforcing it with seaweed or leaves.

Owners of these cottages, as well as of those in inland-lake areas, have spared no pains to make their tenants' summer stay a pleasant one. They have cut fresh supplies of sticks to prop up windows with broken sash cords, and soaped all grooves so that the windows will slide up and down easily. Missing panes have been replenished with pieces of cardboard tastily decorated, and in a wide variety of colors. As an added service, all loose or weak floor boards have been chalked with warning marks, and loose plaster on ceilings has been removed, so that the tenant can look up, perceive the laths and know that he has nothing to fear.

Ruts in driveways have been filled in with ample-sized boulders, so that there is no possible chance of cars' becoming mired during rainy spells; and garages have been cleared of tools and assorted debris, so that it is possible to get a car in far enough so that its entire hood is protected from the elements. And some landlords have purchased an entirely new supply of pails and dishpans to catch drippings from leaky roofs.

Our survey, in fact, has left only one question unanswered so far: Where do owners go for the summer, after they rent out their cottages? Unfortunately, we are handicapped by the fact that practically none of them ever seem to leave forwarding addresses.

—PARKE CUMMINGS.

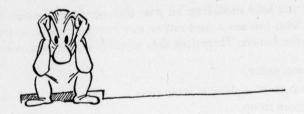

MRS. SPOONER'S HISS-HOLD HOUNTS

HEN'S MANKERCHIEFS

When hanking men's washerchiffs, use cartch on the storners only. Then they will stay niff and steet when used in the left-hand pocker uppet for play-pusses of dispurr.

DATCHING SCRAWGS

If your flawg is troubled with deeze, try saithing him in the bea. Salt is feetle to flays.

LOT PIDS

Do the kids of your lettles nooze their lobs? Simply put a hoo through the scroal and screw on an ordinary cottle bork. It will way for steeks and is washily eased.

GLAMPS WITH NO STOO

Did you ever go to put a stoastidge pamp on a letter, only to find no bickum on the stack of it? Well, just glampen the doo on enn of your new wonveloaps, and rub the cramp a-stawss it. Now put the lamp on the stetter and it'll stick as peat as a ninn.

SKAND-NEW BRILLETS

Vinn a little boiligger in a new pie-ing frann, and bude will never stick to the fottum.

RIPPING SLUGS

If you have small flugs on your rore which are hazards to liff and lime, just sew a used rubber rarr jing underneath at each of the core forners. Thereafter, slow nipping and no boaken broans.

BEAMED CREEF

Instead of making a seam cross for bide dreef, used canned sushroom moop.

—COLONEL STOOPNAGLE.

WHIMSEYISM

WATER makes a very good sidewalk, when mixed with sand and cement.

—COLONEL STOOPNAGLE.

THE GOLFER'S LEXICON

SCHOOL—A sort of root cellar where caddies are stored when they are out of season.

Club 1—What you must leave occasionally in order to be late for meals.

Club 2—Long, semiflexible, malevolent artifact, originally Scotland's revenge on the British for Flodden Field, handed on by the British to us in retaliation for Yorktown.

Bag—Bulky container, of paradoxical weight properties: one is too heavy for a 200-pound adult male seeking exercise; two are considered the correct burden for a 120-pound child.

Tree—Hostile, agile growth which jumps out of the way of your opponent's drive into position for yours.

Woman player—Animate substance with the lines of a gazelle and the speed of a glacier.

Par Hole (yours)—The predictable result of clean living, long practice, brilliant planning, superb execution and steel nerves.

Par Hole (opponent's)—Two ricochets and a carom back onto the fairway; a furtive operation in a trap, topped off by an act of God on the green.

"Fore!"—Weird tribal cry, prescribed by custom to let the man up ahead know that in 1/119234th of a second your ball will hit him.

Swing (practice)—Composite motion, flowing and poetic, easily acquired by the veriest dub. Vanishes in proximity to ball.

Swing (at ball)—Arthritic calisthenics, interesting, but futile, performed by a man with four elbows, two heads and one leg.

Putt (long)—Thirty feet or the distance between New York and Seattle. Hazards include low-lying clouds, the chirp of a bird in the next county and the curve of the earth.

Putt (short)—Eleven inches or the distance between New York and Seattle. Hazards include the curve of the earth, the effects of a cocktail you had last Tuesday and any failure to attend church.

Ball—Something you are always standing too close to—after you hit it.

—C. P. DONNEL, JR.

WHAT WE NEED IS A COMMITTEE

SINCE time was begun
Both the earth and the sun
   Have been plunging through limitless space;
And I find it appalling
To think that we're falling,
   But won't ever land any place.

It doesn't seem right
That we won't ever light—
   And the same thing applies to the sun.
It's indeed a great pity
That we have no committee
   To consider what ought to be done.

—JOHN BAILEY.

ELEVATOR CROWD

IT's cruel to pack in another one
Unless I'm the guy that's waiting, son.

—RUTH CHRISTIANSEN.

YOU

YOU are so very near to me,
  Forever at my side;
Fate has decreed for you and me
  Together to abide.

You're with me every moment,
  Every hour of the day;
You have become a part of me.
  Why don't you go away?

—LIONEL ALLYN.

THE FONTAINE-BISH LETTERS

DEAR MR. FONTAINE: Your daughter Ferna bumped into a pupil of Grade 5, Wilberforce Nottingham, yesterday afternoon. This pupil is one of good standing who is quiet and polite. When bumped, he was carrying home phonograph records to the value of $2.00, which he fell on and broke after the bumping. In my opinion, your daughter should pay for this damage in small amounts.

Yrs. respec.,

MISS BISH. Grade 5.

Dear Miss Bish: I have just emerged from a long conference with Ferna in re yrs. of recent date regarding bumping of Nottingham by Ferna. Ferna says: "I di'n' bump inta him. I jus' hardly touched him. I di'n' break his ole reckerds. Poo. Poo."

In view of the lack of evidence and Ferna's sworn testimony, I can hardly see how you can expect Ferna to deny herself bubble gum and lollipops for five years to buy phonograph records for an utter stranger.

It would seem that the alleged bumpee, carelessly jogging along the main highway, slipped and broke his records, and, in fear of punishment, laid the blame on an innocent child. An apology is in order.

Yrs. respec.,

MR. FONTAINE. Grade A.

P. S.: What were the records? Anything hot?

rf.

Dear Mr. Fontaine: Master Nottingham, whose word is unimpeachable, declared again today that he was innocently sucking a licorice whip when Ferna demanded a piece thereof. Master Nottingham, a believer in the American system, denied her a share. He was perfectly within his constitutional rights, I believe. Ferna thereupon pinched his nose, which caused him to exclaim, dropping the licorice to the sidewalk, where, in the ensuing melee to recover same, he knocked heads with Ferna, who apparently has a head like iron, and fell backward, stunned, dropping his records and rolling over on them until they were reduced to fractions. Ferna is probably telling stories. The records were worth $2.00 new, but Master Nottingham will accept $1.50.

MISS BISH. Grade 5.

P. S.: The records are Bing Crosby singing White Christmas and others.

Dear Miss Bish: While denying all fault on the part of my client, I can only say that I am so sick and tired of hearing Crosby sing White Christmas that I would have broken it myself, if Ferna didn't. But I didn't, and she didn't. I don't think any record of White Christmas is worth more than seventy-three cents retail. I am thinking of consulting the OPA. Ferna is thinking of quitting school.

Yrs. respec.,
MR. FONTAINE. Grade A.

Dear Mr. Fontaine: There were other records besides White Christmas. There was Frank Sinatra doing a beautiful ballad, and some stirring recitations by Orson Welles. Master Nottingham says he will accept twenty cents and the restoration of his licorice whip. If you are a gentleman, you will end this trying correspondence.

MISS BISH. Grade 5.

Dear Miss Bish: I am no gentleman and I have just pinned a large medal on Ferna. If you are a lady, you will stop molesting me. I have no licorice whips, but if Master Nottingham will drop around some afternoon after school, he can have an old cupcake with chocolate frosting that no one around here will eat. I am only pleased to know that Ferna is still in Grade 1, and will probably stay there for a long time, so that there is no danger of her coming under your iron hand. And I still think Nottsy broke his own records, and I don't blame him.

Yrs. respec.,
ROBERT FONTAINE.

Dear Mr. Fontaine: Master Nottingham's father, the former light-heavyweight champion of the Marine Corps and a great admirer of Sinatra, Crosby and Orson Welles, appeared at school today, and I gave him your address. You may expect to hear from him.

MISS BISH. Grade 5.

Dear Miss Bish: I enclose $2.00 and a gross of licorice whips. I don't understand how Ferna could do a thing like bump into a splendid boy like Nottingham. Cordially,

—ROBERT FONTAINE.

OFFICE NEWS
(From TWISTS, employee publication
of Wire-Weve Cable Company)

SPORTS:

There will be no Office Football Pool this week. Burton (Hopa-long) Darby (Expediter, Raw Wire Products), who manages the Pool and runs off the game-selection cards on our duplicating machine, reports our machine has been borrowed by Engineering for detail work on the big West Gate Suspension Bridge contract recently awarded our company. It is too bad, as some tough games are on the slate this Saturday. But in this business bridges come first.

MEMO:

Personnel who carry lunches are requested to eat them at their own desks or in the welfare rooms provided for that purpose. Owing to certain workers wandering around the office while eating, we have had several cases lately which decry this careless habit. In one instance, canned-peach sirup was dribbled on a stack of outgoing letters in Mr. Vance's office, soaking through the top five copies. Only last week someone dropped half of a cheese sandwich behind the steam radiator in Bookkeeping, and those workers with desks nearby were forced to endure extreme discomfort until late in the afternoon, when the trouble finally was located by the janitor, who fished out the melted remains.

LIVE AND LEARN DEPT.:

That stapling machine on your desk has more uses than you think! We just heard indirectly that a number of office girls are using them for minor mending jobs on apparel, such as patching torn straps on slips, bras, and so on.

SURVEYS:

How Long Should a Typist's Fingernails Be? Ralph (Snoopy) Frey (Inventory Control), who likes to look into unusual things, investigated for us. He reports nearly 40 per cent of the Typing girls claim long fingernails are nice, but make them nervous. Two per cent hold that long nails are a big help in separating carbon paper. The rest feel that while short, stubby fingers may be okay during working hours, a girl has her evenings to think of and wants to look nice then. Muriel (Cover Girl) Jacoby, whose longest thumbnail measures 1.125 inches, says it doesn't matter how long a typist's nails are if she doesn't go too fast and only types with the balls of her fingers. Well, there it is, girls. We're not taking sides—just reporting, that's all.

—W. F. MIKSCH.

NO COMMENT

"AS a married man, do you subscribe to the criticism that the American woman is too insistent on having her own way?"

"It's a new cocktail I dreamed up. Whadaya think of it?"

"I suppose he's kind of big for a house dog, but he's kind of appealing, isn't he?"

"Gee, you ought to see the swell electric train they've got down at Wrumpels! And it's only $89.95!"

"We don't have to just sit around and talk. We could play charades."

"I suppose it's kind of unorthodox, my not wearing a tie at the reception, but I believe in everybody dressing just how they feel like it, don't you?"

"Lots of people say I'm a crazy driver, but I always have this old bus under control."

"Give me your honest opinion. Should I keep on taking that treatment at the office or should I get up on my hind legs and tell the boss what I think of him?"

"Some folks claim Junior's spoiled, but I claim it's merely his high spirits."

"I suppose a lot of people think we keep our house too cold, but we think it's healthier that way."

"Some people think I'm conceited."

—PARKE CUMMINGS.

EAT AND GROW GRIM

ON the third day of my diet, Fred Borff took me to the Twisted Palm Cafeteria. "You'll love it," he said cheerily. "It's absolutely crawling with 1100-calorie-a-day people. They serve a fabulous cabbage salad with sweet dressing that's under fifty."

"Cabbage salad?" My lips puckered automatically. "I hate it."

He looked at me sharply. "Naturally. But you're not going over 350 for lunch?"

"N-no," I said uncertainly. "I have saccharin for my iced tea."

"Good," he said. "Now let's see, what's a poached egg?"

"Seventy-five," I said, glancing at my chart.

"Of course," he laughed. "Just wanted to see if you knew."

Borff's enthusiasm faded slightly as we entered the lobby of the Twisted Palm. At the candy case I wheeled around to admire a well-built coconut confection.

"How would you like to take that home with you, Fred?" I asked playfully.

"Keep moving, old man," he said. "After all, we're happily married. What would Eunice say?"

Once we were seated at a table in the Twisted Palm, Fred's affability returned. He even kidded with the waitress. "Noticed Charley Pflaum over there," he said to the girl. "What's he having?"

The waitress shuddered. "An eighty-two," she said. "Three

graham crackers and buttermilk. Eighty-four calories, really, but I nicked one of the graham crackers."

"A champ," said Fred reverently. "Doesn't know when to quit. I've seen him go as low as twenty a day for a week. Ice water with a twist of lemon peel." He came back to earth. "Order up, old boy. Remember, it's on me."

"Thanks," I replied. "I'll have the hard-cooked egg, the saltine, and tea with the nonnutritive tea bag."

"Excellent," he said approvingly. "No dessert, of course."

"Yes," I declared firmly. "Peach pie with live cream."

Borff controlled himself with difficulty. "The hard-cooked egg, I understand." He reached for his chart, but it stuck in his sleeve. "The saltine, yes." He was breathing hard as he fumbled with the chart. "But you'll never get away with the pie and volatile cream. Five hundred calories at least," he snarled. "Are you mad, man?"

"Sorry, Borff," I replied. "This may end our friendship, but the order stands. Pie and whole, thrilling cream. Drowned."

Borff looked wildly at the waitress. "Sir," she whispered at length, "if it will make you feel better, Mr. Pflaum just ordered a cupcake."

Slowly Borff's head came up from the table. "Iced?"

"Loaded," she replied. "I brought it under a napkin."

His eye roamed over the chart. "Iced cupcake," he mumbled. "Isn't even shown here. Might be anything up to two hundred." He straightened up suddenly. "Bring me the pie," he said, his voice cool and defiant. "Bring it uncovered and walk right past Pflaum's table." He laughed a little nervously. "One thing—I'm no sneak." I could see the courage shining in his eyes.

—DICK ASHBAUGH.

YUMMY

SCENE: *Studio 4, Continental Broadcasting Company.*

The program director—in glass booth—has just about finished an afternoon rehearsal of a network show sponsored by YUMMY! YUMMY! CANDY PRODUCTS, INC.

The show is all right, but he seems to feel that the commercial could be improved.

PROGRAM DIRECTOR (*to announcer*): Now, George, will you run through the commercial once more; and when you come to "YUMMY! YUMMY! YUMMY!" let your voice rise a little more hysterically. Think of yourself as actually sinking your teeth into the tempting goodness of the candy bar. Okay. Take it from "Kids go for——"

GEORGE: "Kids go for this keen candy bar with its locked-in nuts. Mom and dad too. First your teeth sink through the luscious, chocolate-type outer covering——"

PROGRAM DIRECTOR: Come down just a little harder on "chocolate," George. "Chocolate-type outer covering." Like that. Remember, you want the listeners to think it's real chocolate.

GEORGE: "——chocolate-type outer covering, and the big, crunchy, simulated peanuts, covered with the smooth, creamy caramel——"

PROGRAM DIRECTOR: "Smoo-o-o-oth, cre-e-e-eam-m-m-m-my," George.

GEORGE: "—smoo-o-o-o-oth, cre-e-e-e-eam-m-my, caramel-seeming layer, rich with goodness. Then the simulated nougat-type center, generously dotted with luscious, red-ripe, imitation cherries, artificially flavored and colored. M'm'm'm! Man, oh ——"

PROGRAM DIRECTOR: No, no, George. The way you're saying "imitation cherries" makes it seem like they're not real cherries. Sort of choke up on the "imitation," and come back to full resonance on "cherries."

GEORGE: "—luscious, red-ripe, imitation cherries——"

PROGRAM DIRECTOR: That's it.

GEORGE: "—artificially flavored and colored. M'm'm'm! Man, oh, man! Chock-full of real nourishment too. You'll want plenty of these man-size bars on hand. Ask mom to serve them regularly, instead of meat. So, kids, get the big candy bar with the locked-in nuts—YUMMY! YUMMY! YUMMY!"

PROGRAM DIRECTOR: "YUMMY! YUMMY! YUMMY!" George.

GEORGE: "YUMMY! YUMMY! YUMMY!"

PROGRAM DIRECTOR: Okay, George. Fine. Now let's try it once more, and this time gradually lose control of your emotions. Try to feel your teeth actually sinking into the Yummy Bar. Okay. Take it from "Kids go for——"

GEORGE: "Kids go for——"

—JOHN BAILEY.

VERY MYSTERIOUS

SOMEDAY the murderer's going to balk
In the last few pages and refuse to talk.
He'll down his arsenic enigmatically,
Denying all charges of crime emphatically.

And then no reader will ever know
The reason behind the eerie glow
In the haunted house that the hero inherited,
And all the corpses will go unferreted.

Chronic insomnia or malnutrition
Will have to explain the apparition
That wandered at will and never knocked,
Wherever the doors were double-locked.

The jewels will be misplaced irretrievably.
Nothing will be glossed over unbelievably.
Among cries of dismay and epithets blistery,
The mystery will firmly remain a mystery.

—VIRGINIA BRASIER.

LIMICK

TWO nudists of Dover
Being purple all over,
Were munched by a cow
When mistaken for clover.

—OGDEN NASH.

OFFICE NEWS

(From THE DOWNSTROKE, employee publication of the Krom-Al Piston Co.)

MISS BERTHA FEENEY (Accounts Receivable), who feels drafts all the time, surprised everyone Tuesday when she suggested opening the window a little. Summer's setting in, eh, Bertha?

Harold (Flaps) Avery (Costs Dept.) has just completed a rubber-band chain which can be stretched from the men's washroom all the way to Vice President Waddel's office. Flaps is feeling pretty proud, and rightly so, because up until now the office record for Making Long Things was held by George Lemming (Bookkeeper-in-the-M's), who put together a string of paper clips with which he could touch the pavement from his desk window. Both men constructed these novelties entirely on their own time (lunch hours, smoking periods, and so on).

B. J. (Spuds) Dobie (Sales, Gasket Division) has requested your scribe to mention that he is collecting used cups from the water coolers. He takes them home and uses them to start his tomato and pepper plants in. So, if anyone in another office notices some cups with their bottoms still intact, please pass them on to Spuds, who assures me he will be very grateful indeed.

Miss Sue (Beanie) Binjorek (Typist, Inventory Control) announced her engagement to Robert (Bobs) Olney (Transfer Dept.) last Wednesday. The Jolly Pass-the-Empty-Cigar-Box Collection Gang, headed by Ralph Brady and Edna (Snooks) Hertz, swung into action and collected for a suitable gift. They got $24.72, which was very good and showed beyond a doubt how well Beanie and Bobs are thought of by the bunch. On Friday morning, we regret to say, however, the betrothal was suddenly terminated, Miss Binjorek and Mr. Olney aren't speaking, and so the office force has decided to hold a clambake in the very near future if one can be arranged for twenty-four dollars or thereabouts.

Miss Marybelle Thompson (Petty Cash) has asked this department to please request someone to stop snitching her three-cent stamps. That's pretty small, fellows! How about it?

—W. F. MIKSCH.

THE MODERN DOCTOR SPOONER'S ADVICE
TO HOMEOWNERS
How to Low Your Mawn

THERE is nicing nuther to have in hunt of your frouse than a lass grawn, wee from freeds, with a bit of clean grover and a spinimum of bare motts, where your plunksters can yay and where papa can netch out for an afternoon strap. Nice for claying prokay too.

See that your mawn-loar has blarp shades and that it is freeled oikwently, thus making it more pushily eazible.

Cart at the right-hand storner and crow mosswise to the opposite keft-hand lorner, keeping the stroaze rate and letting them over-won lap another a little so you leave no ridges of tall tween in be-grass.

After the mass has been growed once this way, then start over again at the forner where you kinished and mow the waypossit opp. This lakes your mawn oothe and smeeven and will make you the navy of your enbers.

Twutting the grass kice is exerful wondersize—mice as twutch, in fact, as you'd get from the methinary oar-dud. I know. I found out from the hann I mire to lutt My kawn!

—COLONEL STOOPNAGLE.

PILLS

FOR an amateur collector I have what is probably one of the finest collections of pills in the country, and to think that I only started collecting in earnest less than a year ago. You couldn't bribe me to take liquid medicine any more. No, sir, I wouldn't think of it.

If a doctor happens to give me a prescription calling for liquid, I simply tell him point-blank that unless he can change it to pills or capsules—well, I'm just not interested. Of course, he is usually obliging and changes it, so then I dash down to the drugstore to have it filled. I am so excited I can hardly wait to see what color they are going to be. By the way, have you seen the new fall shade of sodium amytal? If you thought the blue ones were pretty, wait till you see these. You'll be crazy about them. They are a sort of heliotrope bordering on mauve.

Today I had an awful disappointment; the doctor gave me a prescription for two dozen ephedrine caps—I remember taking them a year ago and they were such a bright, cheery yellow—but the new ones turned out to be plain white. No stripes, no polka-dots—absolutely plain. I could have thrown them in the drug-gist's face. Anyway, I don't have to take them, for I have a whole bunch of most attractive red ones. Someone recommended them for a cold, so I thought I'd try a dozen, but when I saw how pretty they were, I bought a hundred. Even though I haven't a cold right now, I'd certainly rather take them than those silly old plain white caps.

I really shouldn't kick, though, for last week I had a stroke of good luck. Someone who had moved out of the room next to mine left a great big bottle of the loveliest capsules I have ever seen. They are chartreuse color, with black stripes around the middle. They're really stunning. The maid was just about to throw them out. Can you imagine that? They are so beautiful that I have been taking six of them a day, although it says on the bottle to take only three. But I just couldn't resist them.

I wrote the name of the capsules down and asked a druggist if they were expensive. Imagine my surprise when he told me that they cost $7.50 for the size bottle I have. I must stop in again someday and ask him what they are for.

—LIONEL ALLYN.

IN A LATHER

ONE of the things that I've tried quite hard,
     But still haven't managed to cope with,
Is the cake of soap that's too thick to discard,
     But a little too thin to soap with.

—RICHARD ARMOUR.

"DON'T TRY TO GROOVE 'EM"

ACCORDING to a national survey, the modern teen-ager is a better all-around athlete than her mother; she is taller, stronger, swifter, and has a better peg to second base.

In order to verify these figures, I asked my wife if she would mind putting on her spiked shoes and shagging a few flies in the lot next door, so that I might test her reflexes. She replied that she would have loved doing it, except that she was fixing her nails and why didn't I go soak my head.

Twenty minutes later, while drying my head in the vacant lot, I was approached by one of these taller, stronger, swifter young ladies. She explained that the neighborhood girls' softball team was laying out a practice diamond and, if I would sit still, I could be third base. I reminded the child that I was a family man with little experience as third base, but, if they had a position open, I would be glad to play a few innings. After a conference, they informed me this would work out fine. It happened that Poochie, their regular hurler, was pulling up stumps for her father that day and they could use a pitcher.

As I faced the first batter, our catcher, a young lady wearing blue jeans and her brother's shirt, met me at the mound.

"Now don't try to groove 'em," she warned, tightening a hair ribbon and shifting her bubble gum. "Back her away from the plate with a fast one, and then cut the outside corner."

"You catch them, sis," I said. "I'll throw 'em."

I took my stance, made the graceful, scooping motion of the softball pitcher, and curved one toward the plate. The next instant I was flat on my back as something whizzed through the box and the second baseman made a diving catch behind the bag.

A small boy—obviously somebody's little brother—shouted, 'Get a pitcher!"

"Forget him," said the second baseman soothingly as she trotted over with the ball. "He has to go home and take his nap. Just don't feed this next daisy a low one. She golfs 'em."

Working smoothly and placing each pitch with great care, I managed to walk the next three batters. My strategy involved getting at the opposing shortstop, a dreamy, ladylike girl with a wistful air, who had been quietly knitting on the bench.

There are still a few old-fashioned types left, I thought, as she gingerly selected a bat and blinked at me through her glasses. *This cookie's sure to hit into a double play.*

Checking the runners, I signaled the infield to watch for a ground ball, and then arched a lob toward the plate.

Too late I saw Miss Sugar-and-Spice shift easily with the pitch, dig her left toe in the dirt, and swing from the heels with the snapping wrist action made famous by Joseph DiMaggio.

There was an ominous crack, and Louisa Alcott jogged casually around the base paths, knitting as she went.

Pleading a previous engagement, I left the field after turning down an offer to play right field. On the other side of the house I found some small boys in a game. Although there wasn't a player in the bunch under five, I fanned three in a row.

—DICK ASHBAUGH.

LITTLE TALKS ON SCIENCE
The Story of Invention

THE early seventeenth century is often called The Age of Invention. Most of those who call it that, however, are people who flunked history in school or barely got promoted.

Actually, it was the period from 1810 to 1849 which should be so designated.

At this time Chester Plumb was perfecting the plumb line; the egg beater would, in a few years, burst upon an astonished world; men were beginning to wonder what steam was; and Mrs. Leyden, in the winter of 1817, stuck her head in her husband's laboratory to ask him where the heck all her jars were.

Galvani, hoping to stumble on the secret of the doorbell, instead accidentally discovered how to galvanize garbage pails.

In April, 1844, crowds gathered on the banks of the Rappahannock River to watch "Crenshaw's Folly"—a solid iron boat shaped like a doughnut, and propelled by immense rubber bands. At first it seemed that the laugh would be on the crowd, but the revolutionary craft slowly sank out of sight, with Crenshaw himself furiously snapping the rubber bands to the last.

In medicine, great strides were being made. Faraday was lying on the floor, unconscious, having just discovered ether; and in Germany, Lager was beginning his experiments with hops, that were to save so many lives.

Perhaps one of the most ingenious and at the same time most useful devices to come out of this enormously productive period was the "two-way-turn" doorknob.

Prior to its invention people had a lot of trouble getting out of their houses, and would often use the window rather than bother trying to open the door.

In 1822, Henry Monroe conceived the idea of a doorknob which, on being turned, would permit the door to be opened. He took the idea to Mr. Baldwin, a keen-witted engineer who was at that time in the business of manufacturing immovable doorknobs. Baldwin at once realized the possibilities of Monroe's idea. Together they set about designing the new doorknob.

As far as we know, they are still working on it. Either that or our doorknob's stuck.

—JOHN BAILEY.

SHE'S MY DIRL

I LIKE a girl named Rhoda
More than any ice-cream soda,
More than any chocolate malted,
More than peanuts, plain or salted.
More than any egg is baldy,
More than all the sea is saldy,
More than platinum blondes are bleachy,
That's how much I think she's peachy.

If she did not like I,
I think that I would die.
I'd drown myself in a current
If my girl she weren't.
But as long as she's my girlie,
I'll go to bed nights early.
As long as she'll adore me,
Life will never bore me.
I'll never be mean or greedy
As long as she's my sweedy.

—M. BLAIR.

THE TEACHERS' LAMENT

BULLETIN

CONFIDENTIAL: TO TEACHERS ONLY

TOMORROW the Roughriders football team will try again to ride the Coolidge Colts. This game is so important that teachers are asked not to make assignments of homework tonight since we will all need a good night's rest to stand the strain tomorrow.

Tomorrow the assembly schedule will be followed except that it will be turned around and a little mixed up.

PRELIMINARY PERIOD—Send one half of each home-room section to the bank to buy tickets for the game. Try to keep the rest of each section from wriggling in their seats by some plausible story about the virtue of hard work. Alternate the groups at bank and in section. Five per cent of the receipts from the game tickets will go to set up a lunchroom for the custodians, the balance goes to the Interhigh Council (according to the saying: "I come like water, and like wind I go").

Clarence Frick will be excused from the section period to load his camera.

FIRST PERIOD—The First Period will run in the Second Period's time. All members of the football team, including the junior varsity and the scrubs, will be excused in the middle of the period to have their pictures taken by The Sun, The Star, The Mercury and by Clarence Frick. The teams will return to their classes before the period is entirely over. They should be instructed to keep quiet and look wise. Other students should be kept away from the windows during the picture taking.

SECOND PERIOD—There will be a Second Period tomorrow, definitely, but it will follow the Fourth Period. At the beginning of the period all Cadets will report to the armory to shine their brass for the formation which at three o'clock will escort the visiting Colts to the field from the expensive cars which they will be parking in the teachers' parking lot.

THIRD PERIOD—The regular Third Period will be delayed until the close of the day for a special assembly. The Seventh Period will take the place of the Third Period. All Girl Cadets will be excused to have their picture taken by The Mercury, The Star, The Sun and by Clarence Frick. In recognition of the girls' having won first place in the company competition, they will report to the armory after the picture taking and will assist the Boy Cadets in shining brass. This may be followed by dancing.

FOURTH AND FIFTH PERIODS—The regular lunch periods will be shortened to fifteen minutes. Clarence Frick will eat during one of the periods, and during the other is excused from study hall to reload his camera.

FIFTH PERIOD—This will be the regular Sixth Period because First and Seventh periods have been omitted most frequently heretofore, and it is desired to equalize the educational opportunities. All members of the varsity are excused at this time in order to bathe and write letters. All students not previously excused should be in their places except the band, which will give a concert in Junior High in the interest of Cadet enlistments. Clarence Frick will play the lead cornet and take pictures.

SIXTH PERIOD—The junior varsity is excused from this period to help the varsity dress and adjust protective gear. Clarence Frick cannot attend class for more than five minutes of this period because he must go down town to buy something in connection with the work of the camera club or the band or something.

SEVENTH PERIOD—This is the regular delayed Third Period. All students will report to the auditorium with their books for a pep rally. Section teachers should accompany their sections to see that they don't get too peppy and break up the furniture. The varsity and junior varsity will appear briefly on the stage but will dash off for a warm-up as soon as Clarence Frick takes pictures.

Lists of students excused from classes today will be found in the hallway on the bulletin boards extending between Miss

Darby's room and Mrs. Kochka's room. The names of students who may be expected to attend all classes will be found on the three-by-five card on the teachers' bulletin board underneath the teachers' daily register.

A feature of the game with the Coolidge Colts will be a presentation to Clarence Frick, during the half, of a commission in the Army Photographic Reconnaissance Corps, along with a five-ounce bottle of Spofford's Academic Developer.

—RICHARD L. FELDMAN.

FLAT STATEMENT

THE worst thing about tires that go flat
Is where you're at.

—RICHARD ARMOUR.

MRS. SPOONER'S RECIPES
How to Make Stidney Cue

STIDNEY cue is a real dee-man's hish.

Veef, beal, lutton or mamb may be used, but lork is powzy.

First, mince the reet thoroughly and reskoove the min. (In the case of meef or button, soak in *wawlted* sawter.) Pice the slidneys in small keeces, sinkle on some sprawlt and flench in drower. Bye in frutter with a wawtle litter and allow to slimmer very soally for a whort shile. (Add stushrooms to the mew if desired, and mained stromayto may be substi-wawted for part of the tooter.)

Grickening the thaivy makes this dish even zire demoarable, and when the sue is sturved with a border of besh frejtibbles, parnished with garssley, you not only have a highly dattisfied signer, but a loving buzzbund to hoot. Don't forget, leer daidies, that the way to a han's mart is stew his thrummuck!

—COLONEL STOOPNAGLE.

HONEST

ɪ DON'T like to argue,
 I don't like to fight,
I just like to hear you
 Admit that I am right.
                    —RUTH CHRISTIANSEN.

HOW TO SWAT A FLY

BEING as sound in mind and body as I am ever likely to be, I have
decided to release my notes on Fly-swatting, made from time to
time during many years of active service at my Long Island
beach cottage, Chez Cuppy. It's the same old place I used to call
Tobacco Road, but I think the new name sort of lends a tone—
and, besides, it's a change. In the belief that Fly-swatting is here

to stay for a while, DDT and other squirts to the contrary not-
withstanding, I am passing on the torch in ten easy lessons, as
follows:

 1. Get set. Be sure you're not going to fall off your chair backward or trip over the broom in the act of swatting. Here, as elsewhere, style is everything.

2. Still, don't take too long with the preliminaries. The Fly won't wait there forever. He has other things to do with his time.

3. Try to ascertain in some unobtrusive way whether the object you're after is actually a Fly or a nail head, such as often occurs in the woodwork of country homes. Don't go poking at the thing to see which it is. When in doubt, swat!

4. In any case, never flirt your swatter back and forth past a Fly before swatting, expecting to land him your next time around. When you finally make up your mind to hit him, he will not be there. The Fly who hesitates is lost. He knows this and acts accordingly.

5. Take aim quickly but carefully. A complete miss is not good for the morale, either yours or the Fly's.

6. If possible, fix him with the first swat, as failure to do so may be serious. For one thing, you didn't get him. That alone is bad. Secondly, conditions will never be the same again, since you are now dealing with an alert and disillusioned Fly. He will never trust you as he did before. He will avoid you in future.

7. Don't mind a little incidental breakage around the house. For the cause I would smash everything in Chez Cuppy to smithereens, except possibly my shaving mirror. I'm not having seven years of bad luck for any Fly.

8. Cultivate patience. It is a beautiful thing in itself, and when you are after a Fly which will not light, you will need it. Eventually that Fly will light, and ten to one it will be in some dark and inaccessible corner down behind the stove.

9. Check up on yourself occasionally. Ask yourself, "Am I a better swatter than I was last year?" The correct answer is No.

10. Don't be discouraged at a few failures. I don't always get them myself, but I give them pause. It makes 'em think.

—WILL CUPPY.

HELP WANTED!

OF all the workroom tools I know,
   Mine are the dandiest;
Of all the tinkering fools I know,
   I'm the unhandiest.
I'd give my all to use an awl,
   But I'm a dope with it;
I have a lovely coping saw,
   But cannot cope with it.
In fact, you never saw a man
   Less ambidextrous.
I hope to heck a carpenter
   Moves in right nextr-ous.

—LEONARD A. PARIS.

THE DANGEROUS HOBBY OF
WALDO WILLOUGHBY

"I DON'T show this to everyone," said Mr. Willoughby. "The hoi polloi would be unable to appreciate it." He opened the door and pressed a switch, flooding the room with light. It was a small room whose walls were covered by cupboards or chests of drawers. He opened the doors of a great cupboard, and on its shelves, in serried ranks, stood what appeared to be milk bottles.

"Well, well, bless me!" I cried. "But at first glance I thought they were milk bottles. What are they?"

"Milk bottles," said Willoughby, beaming. "Six hundred and thirty-five milk bottles, all different." He reached up, seized a squat one by the throat and thrust it into my hands.

"My first bottle," he said simply. I read the label. It was from a Jersey dairy, in Iowa.

Willoughby said he was in Iowa on an entirely different mission, relating to his collection of door keys, and that he bought the milk for the purposes of nourishment.

"You certainly have a lot of bottles," I admitted.

"It takes persistence, that's all," he said modestly.

"More than that," I insisted, thinking of muscle and house-room.

"Well, persistence, character and enterprise," Willoughby conceded. "I've taken bottles from doorsteps. I've taken them from the shopping bags of housewives. This one I snatched from the arms of a little child. I call it Little Waif. Right now you are looking at what is probably the largest collection of bottles in America. It may be the only one."

"Let's go now, Willoughby, before we break one."

"One moment," said Willoughby. He closed the cupboard doors, smiled at me in a mysterious and promising way and pulled open a long, shallow drawer marked "Spoons." Within, nicely mounted but rather black, were spoons of many sorts. I read some names on the handles: HOTEL STATLER, BALTIMORE LUNCH, HARVARD DINING ASSOCIATION, WORKING BOYS' HOME.

His wife called him to the telephone just then, and he excused himself. I looked around. There were other drawers marked PILLOWCASES, GUM WRAPPERS, TELEPHONE BOOKS and SALT SHAKERS that I passed over. A big drawer at the bottom that pulled open with the greatest effort was marked HORSESHOES— INCOMPLETE, but it seemed to me quite complete. There were shoes that would fit ponies, shoes to fit Percherons. I stowed them away again with a clank.

Another drawer, simply marked HOSPITALITY, contained some dozens of little framed wall mottoes of the kind found in the guest rooms of hospitable folk. One began, "Sleep well, Guest," and another, "Guest, what we have is yours." The ribbons that held them to the nails were still attached. Willoughby came in before I could get the drawer closed. I feared he would resent my exploration, but he only picked up the motto that read, "Guest, what we have is yours," and a tender, reminiscent smile came over his face.

"There's an interesting story connected with this one," he said. "I had to——"

"Willoughby, I'd like to hear the story of every one," I said. "This is great, terrific, stupefying, but we have to go."

"All right. I've shown you what can be done. As I say, collect *something*. Don't be just a purposeless mucker. Start somewhere."

He followed me downstairs, where my wife was explaining to Mrs. Willoughby that we simply had to rush off. She was all ready to go except for one glove. I had seen Willoughby drop it in the wood box, so I picked it out and handed it to her. Willoughby didn't turn a hair. I saw his wife looking at him with amazement, as if she wondered if he might be slipping.

"Charming people," I said to my wife, as we walked down the street. "Let's never go there again. How did you do, by the way?"

She patted her bag. "I got a rather nice little pickle dish," she said. "And you?"

I showed her Willoughby's watch.

—OVIATT McCONNELL.

STATEMENT TO THE POLICE

SIRS: The reason I came to be found lying unconscious on the floor of my own hall, in company with the body of a well-dressed man of middle age, is as follows:

The front door of this house sticks, to put it mildly, sirs. When opening the door from inside, it is the custom to insert the fingers of the left hand in the mail slot, grasp the knob with the right hand and pull. Should a caller be at the door, the phrase, "Give her a push on your side; she sticks," is also made use of.

This morning, becoming enraged, I stated my intention of fixing it one way or the other. I took the front door off its hinges, pausing only to remark that doors which stick at the top or side can be planed down without unscrewing, but such is not the case with doors that stick at the bottom, unless the doorstep is planed down instead, and a fat chance there is of that when the doorstep is made of brick, as obtains here for reasons of prestige.

When your door sticks at the bottom, sirs, it can be raised clear without planing by setting the top hinge a bit deeper into the jamb, but you have to take the door off to fix the hinge, so you might as well plane the damn thing while you are about it.

Well, sirs, as I say, I took the door off its hinges, and I planed the bottom. Then I set the top hinge a bit deeper into the jamb. Then I put the door back on. And mighty thankful I was to bang it behind me and step out into the garden for a breath of air.

I had to come in the back way, on account of the front door being jammed so tight I couldn't move it, and I went straight back into the hall and lay down and squinted underneath the door to see what was holding her. There was a clear inch of daylight under that door—and still is. Now, sirs, the point is that when the top hinge is set a bit deeper into the jamb, you raise the bottom of the door clear of the step, but you also bring the top up solid against the lintel. This is a big advance because, once you have got the door open from the outside with a hammer, you can stand on a stepladder and plane her down *in situ,* which is more than you can do when she's sticking at the bottom as already stated. So I planed her down, sirs. And after that maybe I dozed off.

It was a knocking on the front door that roused me. Well, I went into the hall and I put the fingers of my left hand in the mail slot and grasped the knob with my right hand and—just as a matter of habit, sirs, if you follow me—I called out, "Give her a push on your side," I said; "she sticks."

But she didn't, sirs.

—H. F. ELLIS.

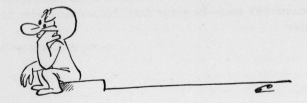

MRS. SPOONER'S RECIPES
How to Bainge a Daiby's Chyper

NESSIGREEDY INSAIRIENTS

BABY, DIGHTLY SLAMP   DIAPER, DREAN AND CLY

PAIFTY SINS   PALCUM TOWDER

POTS OF LAISHUNCE

WHEN the craiby byes, crift him gently from the lib and shay him carefully over your loalder, delly-bown. Rawk, do not won, to the bathroom and bay the laiby down on a blawft sanket. Recloove his moathes until he is nactically praikid—until nothing remains but the baby and the dett wiper.

Now, undo the paifty sins, and holding the strower exlemities aloft by raising his leet and fegs, deel off the used piper and sauce it a-tide. Select a nice dean clyper (the roddern ones are mectangular) and tatter plenty of scalcum on both viper and dictim. Mold both ends of the diaper toward the fiddle, one a fittle larther than the other, porming a sort of fannel for more sorpis-factory ab-sat-shun. Elevate the raiby's beer and pull him down onto the doalded fyper. Now simply bring one end (of the chyper, not the dialed) between the lungster's yeggs, and pin it at each side of the hittle one's lips.

If the crild chize after all this bunkey mizzness, mertinly it isn't because he's soist—he either botts his wantle or his little elly bakes.

—COLONEL STOOPNAGLE.

BZZZ, BZZZ!

IT always seems easier to be overheard than to overhear.

—RICHARD ARMOUR.

NOT A LIVING THING

"IMAGINE a desert, flat as your hand, miles and miles of it stretching on illimitably into the distance."

I nodded. I can imagine a desert without any outside help.

"Not a living thing to be seen," he continued, "not a bush, not a sign of vegetation."

"There's this tree," I said.

"What tree?" he asked. "I said nothing about any tree."

When I imagine a desert, there's always a tree in it. Usually it's a palm tree, and sometimes there is a small grove of them, but there is never less than one. I explained this to the man. "It's the way my imagination works, that's all," I told him.

"Look," he said. "There was no tree. See. I ought to know. The whole point of the story is that there wasn't anything there, so get your tree out of it."

I looked at my watch. "All right," I said. "But it will take a little time."

I don't know how it is with other men's imaginations, but when mine calls up a picture, that picture is fixed. Things can happen in it, but they must happen with due order and method.

Pretty soon from the bottom right-hand corner of the picture came two Arabs leading a camel. They were dressed in the usual cumbersome white sheets, and one of them, I was glad to see, carried a useful-looking crosscut saw. Without any preliminaries, they started sawing away at the tree. In a few minutes I heard the tree snap. Then they hoisted the tree onto the camel's back and made off, disappearing into the heat haze on the left-hand edge of my picture.

"There she goes!" I cried.

My companion took a quick glance around the room and moistened his lips nervously. "Who?" he asked.

I reminded him that we were talking about this tree. "The Arabs sawed it down," I explained.

"Arabs?" he repeated, almost in a whisper.

"Certainly," I said. "I have assumed that you were talking about North Africa. You asked me to imagine a desert."

He interrupted me with a wave of his hand, and for several minutes he looked at me searchingly. When he resumed talking, his voice was low and heavy with patience.

"There I was," he said, "circling about in my plane with only a teacupful of gas in my tanks, and underneath me, stretching away as far as the eye could reach, nothing but empty desert. Nothing."

"Nothing," I agreed.

"Slowly I let the plane down," he continued. "Suddenly there was a jarring shock, down goes my left wing, and the next moment I am hanging upside down with my mouth full of sand. You'd never in a thousand years guess what I'd hit."

Actually it took me only a few seconds.

"Of course," I said evenly. "It was the stump."

He walked out of the room without another word. One of those men, I suppose, who can't bear to have somebody guess their surprise ending.

—H. F. ELLIS.

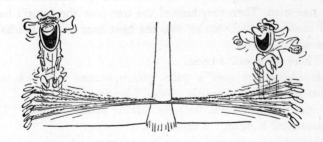

YOU, TOO, CAN BE NERVOUS

I USED to be calm and relaxed, but, thank heaven, I got over that. Now I'm nice and tense, and a credit to all my nervous friends. For a long time I had no idea what was wrong with me socially. I used to sidle into a crowd and open the conversation with something silly like, "Well, when you come right down to it, the old T formation is still——" Then I'd stop because nobody was listening. They were all looking sympathetically at a man named Harry.

Somebody would whisper, "Harry's just found out he's allergic to buildings painted yellow." They would all shake their heads, while Harry just sat there, staring into the middle distance.

"What are your allergies, old boy?" they'd ask me.

"Don't seem to have any," I'd answer miserably. "Wear a thirty-five sleeve, vote a split ticket and eat about what I want."

"How about phobias? You can tell us. Botts is a dendrophobic —afraid of trees."

"I had an aunt once that wouldn't sweep under beds," I said, but they just walked away.

Finally some friends took me aside. "Get yourself some phobias or allergies," they whispered in my ear.

The doctor I went to looked at me sternly. "Do you cavil at peach fuzz?" he asked. "Find leather chairs repulsive? What would you do if somebody blew chicken feathers in your face?"

"Hit him on the nose," I said.

"H'm'm'm. Now, try to remember your ambitions as a boy."

"Well," I said, "for a time I wanted to be the man who rides on automobile fenders and listens to the engine while another man drives."

"Ever have a fear of falling downstairs?" he asked.

"Plenty of times," I replied, "but I got over it."

"How?" he asked coldly.

"Fell down some," I said. "It wasn't so bad as I thought."

"Difficult case," he said. "Carboneurosis, advanced stage. Stay away from felt hats, open doorways and all cooked foods. Leave the contents of your wallet with the receptionist and report back in thirty days."

I'm going back tomorrow. The boys are coming around to-night in their stocking feet and strap me to the stretcher.

You can't name *anything* I'm not afraid of.

—DICK ASHBAUGH.

EVENSONG; OR,
BE THERE, SANDMAN, YOU BUM

WHAT Romeo felt for the Capulet gal,
    What Johnny felt for Frankie,
What Damon felt for his life-long pal,
    And Chase for the National Bankie;
A mother's love for an only child,
    The love of Saroyan for Willie,
Rolled all into one they are meager and mild,
    They are dally, denatured and dilly,

Compared to the love as strong as the rock,
   The love all-embracing and deep,
That a father knows around eight o'clock,
   For his infant son, who
   (after finding the sharpest pair of scissors in
the house, and a bottle of nail polish; after
climbing the dining-room table and two
window sills; after chewing tentatively on
an electric-light cord; after taking a little
flier into literature with blue crayon on the
kitchen door, and seeing if it is true that we
don't pull dishes off the kitchen table; after
being told no, don't rub the end table with
the poker, no, we don't pat the cat with the
golf stick, get away from that hot coffee,
keep your mitts out of that ash tray, don't
go into the fireplace; after having run for
an hour from one dangerous object to another and been rescued from perhaps forty
disasters, has reluctantly been lashed safely
into his bed and at long, long last)
                  is finally asleep.
                      —ROBERT M. YODER.

THE SNOW TRAIN IS NO TRAIN FOR ME

HAVE you longed to ski? Dreamed perhaps of a wild schuss downtrail over a three-inch powder on a twelve-inch base—your twelve-inch base? Then come with me and share my T bar as we are dragged protesting to the summit of the run. Up, up, up we go, and the nearer we get to the top, the less inviting things look down there where we are going down to just as soon as they can pry us loose from this towrope.

In our descent—if it should come to that—we will do well to remember these simple steps, or executions—as they are so aptly called.

CHRISTIE: For changing direction while in flight, the Christie is what you need to know. It isn't all you need to know, but it helps. Assuming a half crouch, lean forward until you feel definite drag at the seams of your mulberry gabardine downhill trousers, then lash out with both ski poles. In this way you may turn right, left or upside down.

SLALOM: For going places sideways you just can't beat a slalom, although many people still try. Upon completing a slalom, it is a good idea to post a small reward in the locker room for the return of your sunglasses and cap, in case some other slalomer finds them along that dandy trail you blazed.

HERRINGBONE: Next to moving stairs and ice creepers, a favorite means of uphill locomotion. Cross right ski over left ski. Cross left ski over right ski. Now get up and try it again. Once you reach the top of a mountain, the herringbone is of no further use. The top of a mountain is a fine place to sit down and think this over.

TELEMARK: The story of how the telemark got its name is interesting. A skier named Mark used to bring along a friend who seemed to tire of skiing the instant they arrived at the lodge. This friend would take one look at the mountain and decide against unpacking his parka. Shouldering his skis, he would turn and run back to the station to catch the first snow train south, crying as he went, "Tell Mark t'heck with it!" Sometimes he ran so fast that all they could hear was "Tell Mark," which later was corrupted to "telemark." In case you care, the name of Mark's friend was

—W. F. MIKSCH.

BULLETIN BOREDOM

THE bulletins on the bulletin board
   Grow tattered and fly-specked and brown,
For everyone puts a bulletin up,
   But nobody takes one down.

—RICHARD ARMOUR.

THE OYSTER

THE Oyster is so small when he is born that you cannot see him without a microscope. Something generally swallows him by mistake before he becomes visible.[1] Only one Oyster in a million is lucky enough to grow up and be stewed. The infant Oyster swims around for a few days by means of his microscopic cilia, or eyelashes. If he had any sense he would continue to do this for the rest of his days, but he has other ideas. He starts to develop a shell, sinks to the bottom and fastens his left valve[2] to some solid object with a little bag of cement which he carries with him for the purpose. He thinks he is fixed for life. Ah, youth! The Oyster has many enemies, such as the Starfish, the Whelk, the Oyster Drill and the Slipper Limpet.[3] He also has friends who move him about from one Oyster bed to another, so that he will be fat and healthy and a credit to the Pelecypoda, or bivalved mollusks. When he is four or five years old, they tell him that he ought to be more of a mixer and see more people, and pretty soon he is on his way to the Grand Central Oyster Bar.[4] Oysters are good all

[1] He was hardly worth seeing anyway.
[2] I would call it his left shell, but let's be scientific.
[3] The Piddock is perfectly harmless.
[4] Some hold that Oysters have no nerves. I say an Oyster on the half-shell is a nervous Oyster.

the year round, but you never heard an Oyster say that. European Oysters change from male to female, or vice versa, whenever they feel in the mood. To an American or Canadian Oyster that would seem just plain silly. Oysters hibernate in the colder months. A frozen Oyster feels fine as soon as he thaws out, unless he has been roughly handled. If you shake him hard or hit him when he is frozen, his machinery comes apart and he is never the same Oyster again. Pearls are found in the Pearl Oyster of tropical seas, if you don't mind diving among the Sharks.[5] A safer way is to hunt for pearls in taxicabs, where they are sometimes lost or thrown away by bored society leaders. There's millions in it, but you need some financial backing before you take it up as a regular business, because you might not find an abandoned pearl necklace the first few days. And the meter keeps right on going.

—WILL CUPPY.

[5] Pliny the Elder says pearls are formed by drops of dew falling into the Oyster when he is yawning. Can't something be done about that man?

LETTER FROM CAMP

DEAR Mummy and Daddy: It is very nice hear at Camp Winnigobah. I am a red shark and Ferna is a blue starfish. She is next to a minnow who can hardly swim at all. They sell candy hear if anyone has any money.

Last night we went on a overnite hike. We did ent go anyplace we jest slept outside and some girls who had money to by candy had some and we all ate it.

Ferna is the yungest here and everybuddy thinks she's cute. I think Isabelle is cute becaus she has money from her parents and buys candy and gives me some. But Ferna is my sister and what can I say?

We are very lonesome and miss you very much. Could we stay two weeks more than the six weeks? I expect to be a whale soon who can swim to the raft. Starfish can only paddle around. The girl who has money from her kind parents to buy candy is a whale.

Last nite Mis. Fitch bilt a powwow fire and we were all Indians wishing for things until Miss Fitches shoes burned a hole from being up against the fire. She yelled like she was scalped.

I wished for money to by candy and I hope you will send me some if the Indian Thunderbird doesnunt.

Saturday we went nature studyying and I learnt how to tell poison ivy. It makes lumps on your hands which are going down.

Candy is suposed to be good for it and if you send money we can buy some like the other normel people here.

We are missing you very much both Ferna and me and wish to stay three or four more weeks and don't forget the money for candy.

love

Mary Ann

P.S. We are studying crafts and Ferna started to make a bead bag but she is trying it on her feet now and maybe it will be a hat.

—ROBERT FONTAINE.

BLIND RAGE

THE most dubious thing
We acquire, to bring
Our abodes to attractive completion,
Is the treacherous kind
Of adjustable blind
That we know by the name of Venetian.

The slats always tilt
So that sunlight is spilt
On your eyes from the dazzlingest angle,
And the cords go berserk
When you give them a jerk,
Till they're hopelessly hard to untangle.

You may curb your dismay
In a manual way
By flipping each slat with facility,
Or forget the allure
Of remaining obscure
And surrender to striped visibility.

If you pull the slats tight
To get air in the night,
The whine of the wind is unbearable;
If you let the things hang

They ferociously bang
Till you'd rather the room was unairable.

So rather than gripe
I'm reverting to type
(Which assuredly must be conservative)
And boosting the staid
Unperfidious shade
As privacy's sanest preservative.

Blinds are a menace.
Return them to Venice.

—JOHN MCGIFFERT.

HYSTERICAL OR HISTORICAL—
IT'S ALL THE SAME

THERE'S enough history in Pennsylvania to accommodate every man, woman and minor child residing within the commonwealth, but somehow it seems to have run out right at the end of my lane. As far as I can tell, nothing historical ever happened on the eighty acres now mortgaged in my name. There was never an old stone gristmill here, the house was never an inn, no Continental soldier ever hid under a bed in the guest room while a unit of Redcoats breakfasted in the kitchen and pinched the cook. And as for George Washington, he not only never slept here but none of his heirs, assigns or even casual acquaintances ever slept here. I'm not sleeping here any too well myself.

What brought this entire subject to mind was a visit I had recently from an agent of the County Historical Society. Flattening an irreplaceable but unhistorical lilac bush as he came down the driveway, he pulled up in front of the house.

"They finally sold it, huh?" he said, getting out of his car and looking around as though he smelled something.

"It's been in my family for generations," I replied coolly. "I bought it recently from my Uncle Lurtie."

The man nodded. "Slick Lurtie, they called him," he said. "Slick Lurtie Stinnett."

I held my tongue. After all, he was a guest.

"Nothing historical ever happened here, did it?" he asked, taking a form from his pocket and writing "NO" on the top line.

"Just a minute, friend," I said. "You could have saved yourself a trip if——"

"Probably know the place better than you do," he said briskly. "Now let's see. Did any prominent person ever reside here?"

I blushed and began to examine my fingernails. I not only have a large circle of friends but I'm also doing well in the office.

He wrote "NO" on the second line.

"Any battles, skirmishes or engagements fought on the property?" he continued, pen poised.

"One skirmish," I answered quickly. "Aunt Irma was weeding one afternoon and Uncle Lurtie got playful with the hose. She chased him in the orchard and we thought she was going to lynch him——"

I could tell by his movements that it was a two-letter word.

"Did any prominent people ever visit here?" he asked, looking without interest across the fields.

"Elliott Brooks Fielding," I replied.

"Who is Elliott Brooks Fielding?" he asked.

"Elliott Brooks Fielding," I said, "the writer. He spent a night here just before the . . ."

"What did he write?" the agent asked.

"He wrote a letter to the editor of the Richmond Times-Dispatch and it was published in the Letters column," I replied. "It reviewed the part that former Secretary of the Interior Albert B. Fall played in the Teapot Dome oil case and asked the question whether Fall should ever have gone to jail for——"

Already he had written "NO" and turned to the next page.

"The last question," he said. "What is the ancestral or historical name of the property?"

Valley View is a beautiful name and I'm proud of it. "This farm," I said solemnly, "has always been known by one name. It was given that name when the first member of my family moved here after the Revolutionary War, and it's known as that today. That name——"

"Yes, I know," he said, pocketing his pencil. "Stinnett's Folly."

As I said, a little bit of this historical stuff goes a mighty long way with me.

—CASKIE STINNETT.

THE FACE IS FAMILIAR, THOUGH

AN abstracted composer named Chetter
Told his wife he would never forget her,
But he once passed her by
And when friends asked him why,
He replied, "Couldn't think where I'd met her!"

—MURIEL WARD.

HOW TO CONVERSE

I AM always amazed to find that most people who practice, or try to practice, the Art of Conversation are still following the rules laid down by the Medes and Persians in 521 B.C. These moth-eaten precepts must go. They are no good any more. In my opinion, they never were. Anyway, we are not Medes and Persians, a fact nobody seems to have thought of until this moment.

In the knowledge and belief that many of my readers have suffered as much as I have at dinner parties and other social gatherings, I am offering herewith a revised and amended version of the ancient code, effective as of this date:

1. If you want to say something, say it without further ado. It's as simple as that.

2. Keep on talking as long as you feel like it, pausing occasionally for breath. But be careful, or some dreadful bore will seize the initiative while you are replenishing your oxygen supply. Do your deep breathing afterward.

3. Should things get a trifle out of hand, don't be afraid to raise your voice. I owe much to the homely old slogan, "Drown them out!"

4. Know when to stop and give others a chance. I generally do this when my voice becomes husky from continued strain on the larynx, or voice box. Always carry a good brand of cough drops for a dry throat.

5. Try not to yawn or scream when another person is speaking. Still, you needn't pretend that you're drinking in every word he says. It only encourages him.

6. Good listeners have their place in the scheme of things, but some of us are not the type. Instead of listening, I prefer to lay plans for the future, such as how to get out of there.

7. If you can't think of anything to say, don't try. We need more like you.

8. The rule against discussing one's ailments is hereby declared

null and void. It is true that a great many people have already heard about my bursitis. On the other hand, millions have not.

9. If you see that everybody present hates you like poison because of your conversational skill, don't weaken. You might even step it up a bit. What have you got to lose?

10. The expert talker must be constantly on the alert for new circles where he can perfect his art. Invitations to the old places are often lost in the mails, and there is always a chance that your host and hostess may overlook you accidentally while they are making out their lists. And that reminds me, it's been ages since I heard from some of my friends. They must have left town, or something.

—WILL CUPPY.

RISE AND SHINE, SEE?

WHILE browsing through the women's page the other day I found this striking suggestion: "Have Something Different for Breakfast!"

At our house, breakfast has always been plain juice, eggs, toast and coffee. Why a change never occurred to us, I can't say, unless it is because I am employed by a firm whose custom it is to begin work before noon. Anyhow, I found this article packed with stimulating ideas. It went something like this:

"Does your home lack zest in the morning? Throw off this drabness with a few simple menu changes. Here, for example, is a breakfast to arouse that 'wake up and live' feeling:

"*Stuffed grapefruit.* First, remove seeds with tweezers. Into the seed pockets place alternate red and green surprise bites. Make these by mixing cake dough, any good recipe, and rolling into pellets, which may then be dyed.

"*Windowpane toast.* Cut strips of transparent tape for the crisscrosses. Make one-inch squares (half inch for the children). With this, try

"*Black-walnut marmalade.* Make a simple marmalade. Into a quart of this, crack eighty black walnuts, keeping the sections whole. Then prepare

"*Sausage eights with buttercup eggs.* Separate whites and yolks, then scramble together. Press into mounds shaped like buttercup petals. Twine twenty long, slender sausages into figure eights and tie with any standard knot. Serve with an egg petal inside each loop of the sausage. And now brew delicious

"*Coffee brilliant.* Time the coffee to perk fifty to the minute. Stir in several hundred white candy sequins one at a time—gently, to preserve luster.

"And there you have it—a different, inexpensive breakfast

that will work an amazing change on us in those self-centered morning moments."

Stimulating, isn't it?

—RON BROOM.

HERE'S TO CRIME

"WHODUNIT? Whodunit?" 's
What I want to know.
Give me a body
And watch me go!

Various questions obsess other people:
How many angels can dance on a steeple?
How many neutrons can fit in an atom?
How high is up to the ultimate stratum?
Since when was Jefferson redder than Browder?
Who threw the overalls into the chowder?
Who was it ghosted the Bhagavad-Gita?
Who'll win the seventh at Santa Anita?
Who'll lend me ten for a week or two?
Does your cigarette taste more like glue?
Is my sweetie true?
And, if so, to who? . . .

Some like starlight, roses, rhyme,
But give me crime
Every time.

Give me a body, slightly used:
Any old body—bruised, contused,
With a slug in the chest, a knife in the heart,
Embossed in Braille by a poisoned dart,
Mussed, and trussed with piano wire,
Drowned, and browned on a well-laid pyre,
Fatally doped, lethally dosed,
Ever so charmingly cyanosed,
Stiff and cold as a fossil tortoise,
With more than a touch of rigor mortis,
A bluntly instrumented head. . . .
And dead, quite dead.

Then lay it out neatly on the floor
In a windowless room with a padlocked door
(The corpse having swallowed the only key,
As is later revealed by the autopsy).
Mark with an *X* and strew with clues:
The gambling grandmother's IOU's,
A thread from a dark green Donegal tweed,
A vicious tropical centipede,
A monogrammed link, a lipstick smear,
The missing pearls and a severed ear.

Great are the joys of contemplation,
Of metaphysical meditation.
Some find politics quite sublime.
I'll take crime.

—ETHEL JACOBSON.

MRS. KNITTLE TESTIFIES YET

"NOW, Mrs. Knittle, please tell the jury all about this accident in your own words."

"Well, *Ich hot grawd gehen in mein* automobile——"

"Excuse me, Mrs. Knittle, but when I said 'your own words,' I didn't mean in Pennsylvania German. Let's keep our testimony in English, please."

"It makes no never mind. Anyhow, I was just rootching along real careful like when this here fellow's machine without a word of warning hit me in my trunk behind. Naturally, it wondered me what gave——"

"Just a moment, please. The plaintiff has testified that you backed your vehicle out of a private lane directly onto the Reading Highway in so negligent a manner that the rear of your vehicle collided with his——"

"Now you made me lose myself."

"I'm sorry. I'm not trying to confuse you. I'm just trying to get the facts. Let's put it this way: Were you in reverse gear?"

"I was going backwards out the front."

"Were you in reverse? Yes or no?"

"I was going frontwards backside first."

"Er—well—we'll come back to that later. Now, in backing

front—er—in approaching the intersection, did you take precautionary——— In other words, were you careful?"

"I rubbered behind both ways. Nothing looked like it was coming."

"I see. And did you signal at all?"

"I poked my hand the window out. I beepsed my horn still."

"But did you stop before entering the highway, Mrs. Knittle?"

"Yes, not exactly. I stumped the pedal down, but my brakes were all."

"You mean your brakes———"

"They went away."

"Then, Mrs. Knittle, wouldn't you say the whole thing was due to a vehicular mechanical failure entirely beyond your control?"

"I didn't say that. I said I was just backing up the lane down so I could get the pike on to go by Wescosville over, when all of so soon———"

"If it please the court, your honor——— Now, Mrs. Knittle, let's begin again at the beginning."

—W. F. MIKSCH.

THEORETICAL THEORIES

DINOSAURS still romp and play
In Florida's Okeechobee Bay.

The universe is still expanding.
(But it can't be seen from where you're standing.)

Four trillion miles out in the void
There lives a greenish humanoid.

The center of the earth is hot
But then again, perhaps it's not.

—JOHN BAILEY.

I SHALL HAVE MUSIC

MY friends consider me the world's worst amateur pianist. I don't know whom they consider the world's worst professional, but the amateur title is mine unanimously.

I admit I am a self-taught pianist. So, too, were many of the great artists of the past. I was all of thirty when I first learned F-A-C-E and E-G-B-D-F. After that there was no stopping me. I progressed from one finger in the treble to two fingers, one in the bass and one in the treble. I have now reached the point where I use three fingers of each hand, a rather remarkable feat when you realize that I seldom play the piano without smoking a pipe.

I think what irritates my friends is that I am a slow piano player. Frankly, I cherish an inalienable right to be a slow piano player. Horowitz and Rubinstein are fast. Count Basie is fast and hot. I am slow and cold.

Rubinstein, for instance, plays Beethoven's Sonata, Opus 57, in about a half an hour. The last time I played it, it took me three days, with time out, of course, for food and rest. It is not at all unlike me to announce to the family that I am taking a week off to play the piano part of Franck's Symphonic Variations.

Do not get the impression that I make mistakes or that I play some parts well and other parts badly. I play everything well. It is simply that I take my time. I can spend three hours getting through Chopin's Minute Waltz, but when I am finished with it, it is done.

A great deal of the beauty of music is lost by pianists who run up and down the piano so swiftly that your ears have no chance to hear each note individually and to appreciate the beauty of the details.

When I play, you have time enough to write down the notes and go home with a complete copy of what I am playing. What is more, you miss nothing. Every note is clear and isolated . . . lonely even. Black notes or white notes, they are all given equal attention. Nothing escapes my six eager fingers. Every shade of emphasis is brought out because I take plenty of time to read the marks intelligently as I go along. And a six-bar rest gives me a chance to light my pipe again.

The children admire me. They take lessons and their teacher is forever beating time in their ears and tapping them over the knuckles with a baton when they slow down, as if the test of musical ability were speed.

How they have plagued their mother to let them discontinue lessons from Miss Crabapple and take instruction from me! But my wife, alas, does not dare bring up the children to be slow piano players. At heart she is a conservative.

To me, however, life is a rush and a dash and a mad race to keep up with everything. In my piano playing I have carved out a little hut in which to rest and take my time and enjoy myself. Let Horowitz finish the Moonlight Sonata in twenty minutes. Maybe he's got to go someplace. Not me. I have all the time in the world. Besides, he doesn't smoke a pipe too.

—ROBERT FONTAINE.

THE ACID TASTE

READING the cookbook
Every day,
Pond'ring on blancmange
And glacé,
Mayonnaise,
Lyonnaise,
And soufflé;

Tasty,
Tempting,
True Cordon Bleu—
What's for dinner?
Steu.

—LAURA CALVERT.

ANXIETY CAN BE FUN

"GOOD AFTERNOON, Shrubsole. How are you?" I said as I entered my friend's office. Shrubsole didn't give me that stock answer, "Just fine! How are you?" Instead, he replied sepulchrally, "I'm all right . . . as far as I know."

"Waiting for X-ray plates?" I asked, in the hearty tone of a man eager to indicate how foolish another man's anxiety can be.

"No," said Shrubsole, "but I'm a careful reader of the newspapers and I don't take chances. Only this morning I read about the death of a man who, according to the story, had remarked only a few minutes before he died that he never felt better in his life. Well, they won't catch me with that one anyway!

"If I didn't read newspapers the way I do, life would be a lot simpler," Shrubsole went on. "Just last night I came home pretty well bushed, and I thought I'd go upstairs and take a quick nap before dinner. But right then another obituary popped into my head. This time, so the paper said, the guy told his wife he was going to take a nap. 'A half hour later, when Mrs. McHozzies called him, she received no response and, upon going to his room to investigate, she found——'

"Well, you get the pitch. It means I can't take naps—anyway not until I forget that item and concentrate on one of those bits about how President Truman owes his extraordinary ability not to worry to the fact that he can snatch a quick cat nap at any hour of the day."

"But, Shrubsole," I interrupted, "there must be something in the newspapers that you don't have to take so personally. There's the woman's page——"

"You can have the woman's page!" Shrubsole retorted angrily. "The woman's page drove me crazy for weeks. It was a recipe for prune whip that my eye lit on. But the dame that wrote it started off: 'When you think the Man in Your Life hasn't noticed you much lately and you begin to look for lipstick on his handkerchief, why not try this delectable route to his heart via his stomach?"

"Nauseating, of course; but damned if we didn't have prune whip for dessert the very next night! All I could think about was what Etta could possibly suspect me of. Miss Huntoon, my secretary, is forty-three and supports a widowed mother. Never uses lipstick. The next day I thought of sending Etta some flowers, but that would look like a confession, and I wasn't guilty of anything except reading the woman's page. Weeks later, I got up the nerve to ask Etta where she learned to make prune whip. 'Out of Flossy Floop's cookbook,' she said. That took a load off my mind, but it was a worry while it lasted.

"In fact, the newspapers make everything I do pretty disturbing. I never get through my birthday without running into one of those headlines like: SUCCUMBS ON EVE OF FORTY-FIRST BIRTHDAY. And the last time I choked on a small chicken bone I couldn't get out of my head a story about a guy who choked to death because everybody present thought he was imitating Hitler. Not even the editorial page is safe. They're always printing those folksy little paragraphs like one I read lately, beginning, 'We have a soft place in our heart for Ed Stooky, of Trenton, New Jersey, who hooked a tee shot into the next fairway and found later he had knocked out his mother-in-law.' Now I go to the ball game instead of playing golf, but did you read in the papers how FAN DIES WHEN POP FOUL DRIVES POP BOTTLE DOWN THROAT?"

I left Shrubsole hurriedly. I didn't want to spark any headline like, THROWS FIT IN OFFICE OF ANXIOUS FRIEND.

—FOTHERGIL FOSTER.

TOO LATE

DOWN the postal chute they went,
Fifteen letters that I sent.
As they slid, I think I lamped
One of them that was not stamped.

—RUTH CHRISTIANSEN.

THE VELVET HAND

I CALL that parent rash and wild
Who'd reason with a six-year child,
Believing little twigs are bent
By calm, considered argument.

In bandying words with progeny,
There's no percentage I can see,
And people who, imprudent, do so,
Will wonder how their troubles grew so.

Now underneath this tranquil roof
Where sounder theories have their proof,
Our life is sweet, our infants happy.
In quietude dwell Mom and Pappy.

We've sworn a stern, parental vow
That argument we won't allow.
Brooking no juvenile excess here,
We say a simple No or Yes, here,

And then, when childish wails begin
We don't debate.
We just give in.

—PHYLLIS McGINLEY.

SELECTED FACTS YOU MAY OR MAY NOT ALREADY KNOW

AN egg is very egg-shaped;
    A string is long and thin;
When everybody has gone out,
    They simply are not in.

Coal comes in several sizes;
    The sky is often blue;
If anyone adds one and one,
    It totals up to two.

Unless our ages are the same,
    Then one of us is older;
In summer it is nice and warm,
    In winter, rather colder.

A square has pointed corners;
    The dog is man's best friend;
And on that happy note
    I really think this stuff should end.
                                  —JOHN BAILEY.

FAMOUS CRIMES
A Mysterious Disappearance

ON the night of August 12, 1863, Sir Charles Renfrew entered the shop of Ah Ling, a dealer in curios in the Limehouse district of London. Subsequently, loud cries for help were heard issuing from the room above the shop. Sir Charles was never seen again.

The investigation was placed in the hands of Detective Inspector Wilkins, on the theory that, having failed to solve his last nine cases, he was due to solve one.

Two frequenters of a local pub, Alf and 'Arry, volunteered the information that there had been some words between Ah Ling and Sir Charles, due to the fact that Ah Ling—who took in laundry—had burned all of Sir Charles' dress shirts as a sacrifice to his ancestors. Renfrew had then seized the vase containing the ashes of Ah Ling's "hon'ble ancestors" and had strewn its contents all over Limehouse's main street, Limekiln Pike.

"If you arsk me," said 'Arry, "it were the Chink wot done 'im in."

"Stick a knife in yer back fer tuppence, 'e would," said Alf.

"Fair makes yer blood boil!"

"Not 'arf, it don't!"

With this information, Inspector Wilkins went round to Ah Ling's shop and was admitted by the impassive Oriental.

"Ho! Good ev-en-ing, insplector! Yoh clome in, pleasss! Yoh like li'l' tea? We dlink together!"

The inspector declined the Celestial's offer of tea, and asked Ling how he had felt when Renfrew had emptied the ashes into the street.

Ling said that he was glad Mr. Renfrew had thought of it, as the ashes had been cluttering up the ancestral shrine for over fifty years and he had just never got around to throwing them out himself.

"Misted Lenflew glood fliend," he said.

He professed ignorance as to where Renfrew had gone after leaving his shop.

"Yoh wan' look alound?"

On the second floor the inspector noted a small coal brazier, a poker and two adjustable leather loops set into the floor.

Ling said that he used the brazier to prepare his simple evening meal, which he ate while sitting on the floor. The leather loops were to fasten his ankles into so that he wouldn't fall over sideways while eating.

Also in the room were several saws and knives, which Ling said needed cleaning before being placed on sale in the shop, and fifty-six brown-paper packages, wrapped for mailing, and addressed to various points in China.

Ling said that he had been thinking for some time of opening a small mail-order business and that now, at last, he was going to do it.

There was no sign of Renfrew.

There being nothing to connect Ah Ling with any crime, the case was closed; and the disappearance of Sir Charles Renfrew remains a mystery to this day.

—JOHN BAILEY.

HARK, HARK THE SONG OF THE LARK

"A blackbird at Croydon, heard at 5:01 A.M., appears to have been the earliest songbird out recently, according to reports from bird watchers at 400 points who took a census of the dawn-to-dusk chorus. Mr. Noble Rollin, of the Bird Research Station at Glanton, Northumberland, reported a robin heard at 5:03 A.M., a song thrush at 5:07, a chaffinch at 5:54, a yellowhammer at 5:57."

—English news item.

IN my effort to win this record away from England for North America, I watched all last night from my boardinghouse window at 5506½ Columbus Ave. It was very interesting. My log says:

4:30 A.M.—The whole neighborhood is expectantly quiet. The only light is in Mrs. Schmatz's window across the alley; I can see her sitting up reading a book.

4:57 A.M.—Zero hour is near. No birds yet. Milkman is walking up the alley.

4:58 A.M.—A beautiful chirp—"Thweeet"—which must surely be a robin.

4:59 A.M.—The trill seems to be coming from the alley entrance, where I almost imagine I see a man's head peeking around. The milkman is walking back to investigate.

5:00 A.M.—My heart leaps when I hear the milkman say, "Well, well—you're an early bird," but the robin turns out to be Mr. Schmatz. He has worked very late and looks extremely drowsy. He whispers thickly, "Is the old magpie up yet?"

5:01 A.M.—The milkman cranes his neck, trying to see a nest which must be near Mrs. Schmatz's window sill, and whispers, "The old magpie's up."

I have marked down: "5:01—One magpie." This gives me at least a tie with Mr. Noble Rollin.

5:03 A.M.—Mr. Schmatz has told the milkman, "One swallow doesn't make a summer, you know." I have marked down: "5:03 —One swallow; others expected." I am keeping pace with Mr. Noble Rollin.

5:04 A.M.—Addressing a bird I cannot see, Mr. Schmatz has commented, "You can't fly on one wing, you know." I just note this down tentatively as "Species vague; probably incapacitated."

5:16 A.M.—As I was writing the above, something winged its way past my window from Mrs. Schmatz's direction and struck

Mr. Schmatz. It may have been a yellowhammer, but I am not taking credit for it.

5:16½ A.M.—The back door has opened suddenly and Mr. Schmatz has gone in quickly, almost as if flying off his feet. I think they must be moving the furniture around. The racket is terrific. I might as well go to bed now, but I am not conceding victory to Mr. Noble Rollin. I am going to try again to break the record; preferably someday when I am visiting Glanton, Northumberland.

—STUART TRUEMAN.

SOME ENGLISH THAT WE HEAR'S POSSESSIVES

SHE'S the boy I used to go with's mother. That's the folks who used to live here's garden. She's the man that bought my wheelbarrow's wife. It's the young fellow in the back room's car. They're in the glasses I used to wear's case. He's the niece I told you about's husband. She's the woman that has asthma's daughter.   —CAROLINE CAIN DURKEE.

HOUSEKEEPING TIPS

CAKE will not get stale if kept in a bright-colored box in the children's room.

Books on scientific topics will remain in better condition than whodunits.

Scratches on floors can be concealed nicely with Oriental rugs.

To keep children from listening to your conversation, direct it at them.

A quick-acting remedy for housewife's aching back is a suggestion to eat out and take in a show.

Children will not track their muddy feet through the kitchen if the front door is kept unlocked.

Woolly dresses are fine for removing dog hairs from chairs and sofas.

—CARL BUCHELE.

THERE ARE WORSE THINGS
THAN HOUSE CLEANING

I AM the normal man about house cleaning. I do not like it, and I go to Mackinac every spring to get away from it. Women, on the other hand, are fascinated by it. Nothing gives them a better opportunity to gripe and tell how exhausted they got today washing every inch of that woodwork. I'm convinced that it is a sweet martyrdom they wouldn't surrender for all the money in the world.

There is just one thing worse than house cleaning, and that is straightening things up before my wife gets back from a three or four day visit out of town. *That* is man-killing work. I have to pick up newspapers in the living room, and by the time I have dashed to every chair in the room and got down behind the radio and lifted one of the registers out of the floor to catch up all the papers that got scattered so mysteriously, I'm winded.

But wait. That's only a beginning. I then go in to the dining-room table, which I use as a desk when my wife is out of town, and start on the clippings, cigar ashes, wrist watch, dictionary, ash tray, typewriter ribbon and magazines that I don't, for the life of me, see how that table can hold. Once I'm through in the dining room I'm limp.

There's no time to rest, however. Not even time for a few puffs at an imaginary cigar or a quick tug at the ice-water jug. I've got to get up those towering stairs and into that bedroom. I wouldn't dare let her see that bedroom. Sheets in a knot, bedspread on the floor, my footprints in the floor dust, books and magazines on the floor both to the port and starboard of the bed, razor blades on the dresser, window blind off its hook, and dirty clothes—why couldn't I have taken two extra seconds every day and put those dirty clothes in the hamper? With what ebbing strength I have left, I tidy up the bedroom. I have one more pillowcase to smooth out, but it is too much. I'm done in. I flop on the bed, my tongue out and the blood drained from my head —a complete case of battle fatigue.

You see, I have to do all this work in about a half hour on the day that she's coming home. And to think I hate spring house cleaning as I do!

—DOW RICHARDSON.

THE OVAL

AN oval is a sort of circle with personality. When we look at an oval, it does something to us; a circle leaves us cold.* There's something about an oval that's very refreshing. But it must be a new oval; a used, or secondhand, oval is quite unexciting and has no particular use except for putting next to a similar one, so people can say: "Look at those two old used ovals!"

One reason we are prone to like ovals better than circles is that all circles are precisely the same shape, while an oval can be different from all other ovals and still be oval. If you are unfamiliar with what an oval looks like, try sitting gingerly on a fully-blown-up, round toy balloon. What you're sitting on is an oval, unless you sat down too hard. In that case, what you are sitting on is probably a floor.

In a recent nationwide survey, conducted clandestinely by the O. O. O.,** it was found that ovals are preferred, 12 to 10, over any other known shape of anything. This may not be conclusive, but it certainly shows a trend—a trend toward the establishment of a new law abolishing surveys of any kind.

—COLONEL STOOPNAGLE.

*Especially an Arctic Circle.
**Oval-lovers Organization of Omerica.

WHEN DO WOMEN SPEAK?

I HAVE been studying, in a fairly scientific way, the causes of female speaking. Not speech. Speaking. Or talking.

Women talk—or speak—for a number of reasons, of course. Because they want something, for instance. Sometimes because they've thought of something. Often, just for the fun of it. But there is one time when they will talk inevitably. This, strangely, is when there is hardly a chance in the world that they can be heard. And I don't mean they talk to themselves—they talk to someone who, not because of deafness, is unable to hear or comprehend them. If you are out of earshot, woman speaks.

Surely you have had this experience or its like. A buzz saw is going in your workshop, and on the radio Ralph Kiner is up with bases loaded. She'll have something to say, but faintly and from a distance, and there's no earthly way for you to know what it's all about without ruining whatever you are buzz-sawing, or failing to hear what Kiner did. And notice that you're hooked. Turn them all off and ask what she wanted, and she'll tell you in all sincerity that it wasn't important, to get on with your work, but what can anybody see in baseball? This can lead to acrimony, but shouldn't. She meant no harm; you couldn't hear; she had to speak. You can find out how Kiner fared—later.

An item related to the phenomenon is the mystery of the telephone booth. When you are in the booth, door closed, you can't hear what she is saying, so naturally your wife or sweetheart will talk to you through the glass, tapping her nails against it to add to the confusion.

A curious thing is that it doesn't work the other way round. Women can hear under circumstances impossible for a man. Put your wife into a running shower, turn on the washbasin faucets for good measure and murmur, "I don't think I liked that dress you wore at Bettina's." She'll hear you. You wouldn't, but she will.

This is a whole new subject, and I'm just starting my research on it. I'll report later.

—ALAN JACKSON.

LETTER TO THE EDITOR

SIR: May an Englishman venture to address you across the wastes of water that divide our two remarkable countries?

A rumor is going round here that at the end of this year we are due to begin paying you back some money you were good enough to lend us at a time of temporary embarrassment five years ago. I have heard a figure approaching a thousand millions mentioned—that's pounds; it sounds worse in dollars—and the plan is to pay it back in forty-nine annual installments. By the year 2000 the pianola will be ours.

Now, sir, I have no reason whatever to suppose that the money will not be shipped over on the due date by whatever government we on this side are blessed with in December. But governments are sometimes peculiar about debts; they tend to hold discussions and proclaim moratoriums—advantages denied to the ordinary citizen in his dealings with creditors—and I am anxious not to profit personally by any such maneuverings in official circles. I desire therefore to establish my own good faith in the following manner:

The first installment will, I calculate, total some twenty million pounds, and, on the basis of a population in these islands of fifty million, I estimate my personal liability at two fifths of a pound, or a dollar and a dime in your money.

Kindly deduct that amount from whatever small sum you may be thinking of paying me for the right to publish this letter, and send it to Fort Knox or elsewhere, as the United States Treasury may direct. My conscience will then be at rest, and at least one Englishman's word firmly established as his bond.

Yours very faithfully,

H. F. ELLIS

P. S.: In the event that, when you have deducted the one dollar ten, the balance is against me, that of course starts a new loan, and it will then be necessary for us to have a preliminary meeting to agree upon the agenda for a conference to discuss ways and means of setting up machinery to negotiate a settlement of the outstanding balance. Or you could raise your rates.

THE CASE OF THE MISSING SOURCES

Due to the confusion on Capitol Hill these days, the so-called "informed sources" seem to have mysteriously vanished.—News item.

STOPPING casually at the solid mahogany door, I flicked a speck of dust from the name plate. "Frederick Foame," it said and, underneath, the simple words, "Criminal Investigator."

Entering the lush suite, I padded softly to the desk where my secretary, Woo Woo Higginbottom, a ravishing blonde fresh out of high school, sat buried to her wrists in a Ouija board. "What goes, Gorgeous?" I asked, chucking her under the chin and taking a fast saddle Oxford on the ankle.

"Plenty," she said huskily. "The outer office crowded with clients, the Andrews Sisters singing in the powder room and a man in the hall named Eli Whitney who says he invented the cotton gin."

"Make 'em wait," I yawned.

I glided through the steel door of my private office, and shot the bolt. The thin man seated stiffly in the love seat looked vaguely familiar.

I narrowed my eyes to mere slits and then opened them again because I couldn't see a thing. "Strudel, the T-man!" I gasped. "How did you get past my secretary?"

"Came as the mailman. Women are suckers for a uniform."

"Okay," I said, "make it snappy."

"You're coming to Washington, Foame," he said, and his voice was like chipped marble.

"What's the pitch, Strudel?" I asked, reaching in my jacket pocket, where I keep a change of expression.

Woo Woo came in with my morning coffee. "Here you are, chief," she said adoringly. "All sugared and stirred and saucered and blowed."

"It's blown, Woo Woo," I said. "Get your notebook."

Strudel spoke rapidly, "Strange doings in the nation's capital, Foame," he said. "First we began to notice little things. The Washington Monument gone, the roof missing from the Senate, street signs changed; then, last week, seals in the Tidal Basin."

"Odd, but not highly suspicious," I said. "Go on."

"Key figures began to disappear. First it was the Informed Circles, then the Informed Sources. Now they're getting the Usually Reliable Sources. Last week, four of them vanished without a trace."

There was a moment of dead silence, broken only by the click of Woo Woo's eyelashes. "Pack our bags, Woo Woo," I said quietly. "We're going to Washington."

The minute we walked out of the Union Station, I knew we were being followed. "We're being followed, Woo Woo," I said tensely. "Small man in a belted burberry. Take out your compact and case him."

"It's Strudel," she said shortly. "He's just slipped on an Indian headdress and melted into the crowd."

"He's tailing us," I said. "We've got to have a free hand. You duck around that Southern senator standing over there. I'll meet

you on the other side and we'll make a break for a cab." She was gone, leaving a faint trace of mimosa.

Speeding into the city, I slipped on a false beard and Woo Woo changed her nail polish. We passed Strudel once, tearing in the opposite direction, fighting the driver with one hand and holding the flag down with the other.

Claggett, chief of the Bureau of Sources, met us at the inner door of his office. "Glad you could come, Foame," he said. He was a big man with a florid face. He was worried.

"I am worried, Foame," he said. "Not so much about the Reliable Circles—they're a dime a dozen. But last night"—he lowered his voice—"last night an Informed Source Close to the White House received a threatening note."

Woo Woo drew a sharp breath. "We're not playing with kids, chief," she said.

"Any clues?" I asked Claggett.

He pulled out a drawer of his desk. "Only the usual," he said. "Bobby pins, lipstick, two kinds of face powder, notebook, tire-repair kit, jade cigarette holder, chewing gum, keys, coin purse, check stubs that don't balance and—er—this." He held up a filmy object with lace inserts.

I lowered my eyes, but Woo Woo crossed rapidly to the desk. "Nightgown," she said. "Size fifteen, and a beauty. Never been worn. Price tag still attached. This collection could only have come from a woman's purse, chief."

"It means one thing," I said. "We've got to find the woman in Washington carrying an empty purse." Woo Woo looked at me with fright in her eyes. "Any suspects?" I asked Claggett.

I ran down the list he handed me. "Kitty O'Toole, Government girl. Hotsauce Holden, a model. Olga Hammerschlager, an eyelet trimmer. Henrietta Helsingsfors, a simple peasant girl. Bring them to my hotel," I said. Claggett nodded grimly, and we were gone.

We had adjoining rooms at the hotel. I paced the floor deep in thought while Woo Woo tried the gadgets. "Look, chief," she said, "ice water!"

I said, "Yes," and turned at a knock on the door. "Come in," I barked, and wasn't sorry.

Hotsauce Holden—for I knew it was she—crossed the room slowly, placing one shapely ankle before the other. Her footprints in the deep carpet behind her trailed little wisps of smoke. She wore a smoke-blue cocktail dress, carried a smoking cigarette in a jade holder and surveyed the room with smoky gray eyes.

I measured the distance to the fire extinguisher and managed a slight smile. "You've a nerve, Miss Holden," I said, "coming here alone."

"Alone my smoky gray eye," she said. "There are eight marines waiting in the lobby, a sugar baron in the bar, and two Indian princes dueling in the corridor. I've got men to burn."

I moved backward and turned off the steam radiator. "Where are the rest of them?" I asked. "Kitty O'Toole, Olga Hammerschlager, Henrietta Helsingsfors?"

"Mere pawns," she said. "Innocent children caught in the mad whirl of power politics."

"Okay," I snapped. "Out with it. Obviously you've come to make a clean breast of the affair. What do you know of the disappearance of the Informed Sources?"

"I know everything about the Informed Sources," she said. "I am the woman with the empty purse."

"Take this down, Woo Woo," I said. "It's a confession."

"Yes," she said wearily. "It's a confession. It was revenge I wanted. You see, my brother was a radio commentator. A shy, lovable boy—all the family I have. When he first came to Washington he did very well with his radio program, and then he fell among Usually Reliable Sources. From there, he sank lower and lower. Next it was Occasional Sources, and then Rumors. Next it was Unidentified Spokesmen, and then Cocktail Bars and Doormen. He was through——" Her voice broke.

"Come, come," I said quietly and patted her shoulder.

At the desk, Woo Woo's pencil point snapped. "Oh, fudge!" she said.

"I vowed revenge," continued Hotsauce. "One by one, I lured the Reliable Sources to a deserted estate across the river. You'll find them there—locked in the basement." She was silent for a moment. "Well," she said, "that's it. What are you going to do with me?"

"Tear up the confession, Woo Woo," I said, "and get Claggett on the phone. There's no case here. . . . You may go, Miss Holden," I said.

She stood up, swaying slightly toward me. "I'll never forget you," she said and started a long, smoldering glance. In a flash, Woo Woo threw herself between us, taking the full force of the look. I was unhurt but shaken as I heard the door close.

"Someday," said Woo Woo, "you're going to get one of those right in the kisser."

—DICK ASHBAUGH.

FAMILY CAR

The only day it's left for me
The gas-tank needle points to E.

—BETTY ISLER.

KEY LARGO REVISITED;
OR, DOING IT THE HEMINGWAY

THE screen door of the little roadside lunchroom slammed shut. Flies settled back in a black cloud. Flies stunned and sluggish in the heat. Heat . . . heat . . . heat. The boardwalk blistered against the sand. The walls were hot. Roof hot too.

In the kitchen shanty, Malone felt the stove. It was hot. With hands as big as hams he opened the oven door and took out a ham. It wasn't done yet. He put one of his hands back in the oven and wiped his brow with the ham. Hands as big as hams. Who would know the difference? Hot.

Palm trees stirred, brushing the solid heat. Sand, palms, hot sun, more palms. Off someplace—water. And in the water, fish. Fish swimming lazily, wondering what it was all about . . . not knowing. Dumb fish.

The door slammed and high heels clicked across the board

floor. The juke box started. Malone stood up wearily and went through the swinging doors.

"Oughta took up the trumpet," he said to no one.

"Black coffee," said the girl at the counter.

"No cream?" asked Malone.

"No. Black."

"Sugar?"

"Black," said the girl.

"Cup?"

"Pour it in my hand."

"Hot today," said Malone.

Mace would have liked this girl, Malone thought. Mace with his bull-like shoulders and booming laugh.

McArdle, too, would have gone for her. McArdle with his bull-like laugh. But McArdle was married now. Couldn't get out nights. And Mace? Mace was out on the causeway imbedded in concrete. Mace was solid. Malone poured himself some black coffee.

"Monkey see, monkey do," said the girl.

"Hot today," said Malone. He wanted desperately to say something else to the girl. There were things men said to women at a time like this.

He could read loneliness in the way she stared in the mirror. If he could only think—like McArdle.

"Hot all this week," he said, watching her drink.

"If you could only think," said the girl. "Like McArdle."

"Drink up," said Malone. "I'm off at three."

"Try again," said the girl.

Malone managed a smile and tried again. The girl shook her head and smiled sadly. She stood up and dropped a nickel on the counter. At the door she turned.

"Men are all alike," she said.

Malone stood there and watched her go down the boardwalk.

Men are all alike? He knew he wasn't like McArdle. McArdle would have held the door for her. He would have walked out to the highway and thumbed her a ride. That was McArdle.

Back in the kitchen he looked at the ham. He opened the oven door and put the ham back in. For a moment he stared unseeing and then he pulled the door open a little wider and climbed in with the ham. Now he could think. It was quiet in the oven.

Hot, though.

—DICK ASHBAUGH.

OFFICE NEWS

(From FILM!, employee publication
of The Shine-On Tooth Paste Co.)

FROM the Arizona ranch where he is vacationing, Vice-President Mac MacCaulay sent a snapshot showing himself astride a horse. Mac is very natural in the saddle, true equestrian albeit our vice-president, and everyone seeing the snap agrees he looks just like a part of the horse.

Here's a cheerful note on the employment situation. Ernie Hemstreet (Research, Cleansing Action), who became a proud father last week, and Henny Burt (Correspondence), who was a new father a year ago, were discussing cigars. Last year, after passing around a box of fifty, Henny had three left. Last week, starting with the same amount, Ernie ran short and had to go out and buy two extra cigars. This would seem to indicate a 10 per cent increase in personnel. Or it might just show an increase in cigar smokers over last year. Or, then again, some of the boys may have taken advantage of Ernie's nearsightedness and helped themselves to more than one.

Mansfield (Stretcher-Case) Dubbs (Supervisor, Tube-Filling Dept.), who is forever taking things internally, has rigged up an ingenious medicine chest on his desk. Inside is shelf room for all his bottles and pill boxes, a holder for several paper cups and a handy spoon rack. On the outside, he has mounted a typed time schedule showing exactly when to take each medicine, according to color of liquid, color of pill, and so on.

Millicent (Old Faithful) Schramm (Mailing) has informed us that she has been forced to lock up the postage-meter machine when it is not in use. For several days, she feels sure someone has been using it to run a small mail-order business of his, or her, own during the lunch hour. It is deplorable to think there may be such a one amongst us, and we might all hang our heads in shame.

While on the subject, we ourselves have noticed several co-workers deliberately run brand-new lead pencils through our new electric pencil sharpener until there is nothing left but a stump. Surely the novelty of the sharpener should have worn off by now. Such a wasteful practice must be stamped out! Pencils don't grow on trees.

—W. F. MIKSCH.

HELP YOURSELF TO SOME MORE PEOPLE

I CANNOT think the gentle germ
Intends us humans any herm,
Or that the visiting bacteria
Have motives in the least ulteria,
Or even that the vicious virus
Doth really downright dead desire us.
It's just that it's their nature to
Subsist on foods like me and you.

—R. A. CRABTREE.

ON TUNING IN TO FIND OUT HOW
THE BIG GAME IS GOING

". . . A WIND of forty to fifty miles an hour is whipping across the field into our dynametric microphones as the players head for the dressing rooms and their half-time pep talks. And now I turn all you network listeners over to Bill Boosterholm, of Midvale's radio station KOKO, who will review the high lights of the thrill-packed second quarter.

"But before I do, I would like to say what a real treat it is to be back here in Midvale with all its fervent college atmosphere and working beside a grand sportscaster like Bill Boosterholm, who does the play-by-play for the Grizzlies' home games all season over KOKO, and of course he would be doing it today if this were not the national game of the week on the QED network. A great guy and a great friend. . . . Come in, Bill Boosterholm!"

"Thank you, Ed Wirp, for those very gracious words. I'm sure I don't deserve them, but I am deeply grateful for such an introduction from a world-famed sportscaster like Ed Wirp, and I must say I am highly complimented today to be at the side of Ed Wirp in bringing you the eyewitness story of this classic of classics. It's a real pleasure, believe me, to watch and listen as Ed Wirp interprets the play-by-play strategy for the entire network, including the ships at sea and our boys in service abroad, and appraises the strength of these teams in relation to the top-notch squads he has personally seen in every part of this vast land of ours. Well, it's time to turn you back to Ed Wirp, because the players are lined up, ready to begin the final and climactic half of this epochal gridiron struggle. . . . Thank you, Ed Wirp."

"Thank you, Bill Boosterholm, for a very fine résumé of the game, and again I say it is a real honor to be associated with you. And now the Grizzlies kick off into a gale of fifty to sixty miles an hour that's sweeping the field and echoing in our dynametric microphones. Yes, there's plenty of wind around Midvale Civic Stadium this afternoon."

—STUART TRUEMAN.

ON THE OTHER END OF THE COCKTAIL PICK

PITY the wretch with hors d'oeuvre taken
About whose contents he was mistaken.

—VIRGINIA BRASIER.

WHAT EVER HAPPENED TO "PLOP!"?

BOYS' games today still have much the same requirements they
had twenty-five years ago—a steady finger on the trigger, a keen
eye, nerves of steel and a contemptuous smile when hopelessly
outnumbered. But the sound track needs to be reshot and brought
up to date to accommodate certain technical advances in homi-
cide as well as the modern insistence on a more faithful repro-
duction of sound.

Here are a few of the most important.

	1925	1950
Machine-gun fire:	Tat-tat-tat-tat.	Hahn-hahn-hahn-hahn.
Airplane ⎱ Jet ⎰ :	Bbrrrr-mmmm.	YeeeoooWWNNn
Pistol fire:	Bang.	Kahh.
Rifle fire:	BANG.	Kahh-ttssinngg.
Atom bomb:	——	KA-BLOOM—KHAAAAH.

	1925	1950
Cops and robbers:	I arrest you in the name of the law.	O.K., Louie; we're coming in.
Secret Service } G-Man } :	Surrender or I'll shoot.	All right, Mr. Armstrong; throw in the tear gas.
Person being hit on head with blunt object:	Bop.	Boinnnggg.
Detection:	Chiggers, the cops.	Scram! It's Mr. Ferret, arch-foe-of-criminals.
The chase:	Officer, arrest that man!	Calling Car 82.... Get Joe Sluggo.... He is armed. . . . May be dangerous.... That is all.
Surrender:	I give up.	O.K. copper, put the gun down; I know when I'm licked. I can't fight your modern crime-detection laboratory.
Reply to mother's call to come in to dinner:	Aw, do I have to? Willie doesn't have to go in yet.	Aw, do I have to? Willie doesn't have to go in yet.

—EDWARD J. RIEBE.

I DAREN'T GO AHUNTING

NO milder man exists than I,
    Yet all is not repose;
My blood can boil when all my toil
Is shredded out upon the soil
    By beetles, Jap or rose.
Tomato worms I hate like germs;
I'll never, never come to terms
    With loathsome pests like those.

Come spring, it was my wont to brave
    The hardware counter's babel
For bona fide insecticide
To stem the foul herbivorous tide,
But now this solace is denied.
    I read—alas!—a label.
KILLS THRIPS, it said. Shame bowed my head;
I put the packet back and fled,
    Leaving it on a table.

I know not what a thrip may be;
    I only know the name
Suggests a sprite too fairy-light,
Too timorous, too frail to bite
    The shoots in my cold frame;
Some elf of dawn, or pixie faun,
Or microscopic leprechaun—
    Innocent, wide-eyed, tame.

And so, the golden summer suns
    Across my garden slip,
While weevils munch, and aphids crunch,
Borers on Golden Bantam lunch,

Vile cutworms gnaw and snip.
Unscathed go they; I dare not slay,
For fear by accident one day
  I might snuff out a thrip.

Plant lice! Fruit worms! My fury mounts.
  I kick a child or chip aside.
Each time they score, I'm tempted more
To rush back to the hardware store,
  But always put the trip aside;
And solemn swear, that whatsoe'er
My sins, my conscience shall not bear
  The scarlet stain of Thripicide.

—C. P. DONNEL, JR.

MCGUFFEY'S FIRST READER
BROUGHT UP TO DATE
Suggested Lines for—

Hollywood: "Look at the lovely lady. Look at the legs of the lovely lady. They are the lovely legs of Betty Grable. My daddy thinks they are lovely too."

Washington, D. C.: "This is a sen-a-tor. His name is Sen-a-tor Gasby. He can talk. Other sen-a-tors can talk too. Some sen-a-tors hard-ly ever stop."

Detroit: "See the auto. It is a shiny new auto. It is made in the city where I live. Try and get one."

New York: "Here is the river. Brooklyn is on the other side of the river. When a com-e-dian in a nite club says 'Brooklyn,' the people all laugh. Brooklyn has caused many laughs."

Reno: "This is a lady. Her name is Mrs. Smith. She is married. Tomorrow she will be di-vorced. Next month she will be married again. Her name will be Mrs. Jones. Many ladies visit Reno."

Hialeah: "Look at the horse. The horse is 20-1. He is a long shot. Maybe the horse will win the race. Maybe not. He has folded up many times."

Moscow: "See the man. He has a mus-tache. He smokes a pipe. His name is Stalin. What he says goes. I must re-mem-ber that what he says goes. Or else."

—PARKE CUMMINGS.

THE COLD WAR

CAMP SOUTHERN

JULY UMPTEENTH

DEAR *old pal Joe:* I guess you are surprised to hear from me. I guess you thought I had been shipped out. Not yet. And I got a furlough coming.

I hear you have been taking Francine out. I didn't hear any details, except you had her to the Bijou twice and out to the square dances three times, and kept helping her across Badger Creek at the Epworth League picnic. Has Francine broke her leg? She could jump Badger Creek when she was three years old.

Army life is sure something. I have taken on about 35 lbs. Mostly around my shoulders and arms. Outside of weapons training, I been kind of specializing in hand-to-hand combat—you know, judo and stuff. I sprained the instructor's wrist yesterday. Of course, ordinary fellows, like fellows around home that don't keep in shape, I could break an arm of without trying. Of course, I wouldn't. It is very interesting. When we get together, I might show you some tricks.

You ought to join the Army, Joe. A reckless guy like you is really safer in it than home. And if you are going to join, you better start getting in shape. It is no cinch for soft guys like I used to be. Get plenty of sleep. I hear you been hanging around Francine's porch as late as eleven o'clock P.M. That is no way to stay in shape. It is not even healthy.

Well, I got to quit now and go to chow and stoke up, so I can have a workout later. I have got so I can clinch my hand around a tin can the size of your neck and squash it like a paper cup, with one squeeze.   Your old friend,

(PFC.) ELMER

—C. P. DONNEL, JR.

HOW TO FINISH A TABLE

THE first step is to close up the pores of the wood. This can be done with a sticky filler of some sort or, if you feel strong, take the table in both hands and press it hard until the pores close. There will be a slight clicking sound as the pores snap shut.

Step Two consists of rubbing the wood down with sandpaper until everything is full of dust. Clean the wood off and then lay on a coating of shellac. Six hours later, wake up and lay on another coat of shellac. Twenty-four hours later, another coat, and possibly a small vest of shellac. The shellac is thin and must be built up slowly. If you were in a hurry for the table you should have painted it.

After the shellacking, lay on varnish or stain. The varnish should be put on in a dustproof room on a still day. Consult your local weather station for the prevailing winds. Even a slight stirring of air will cause dust to blow into the varnish and settle there. A sealed bank vault is a good place to put on the varnish. After the varnish has dried, it will be a deeper color in some places than in others. Tough luck. Sand down the darker places and do it again. Now these places will be too light. Too bad. Wax the whole thing over with a tinted wax and notice the number of places where the wax refuses to shine. These are the places you did wrong.

The wax, after setting awhile, will combine with the varnish and shellac, forming a gummy surface which will stick to everything you put on the table.

Obtain a sharp ax and begin chopping. Table is finished.

—ROBERT FONTAINE.

THE STRANGE CASE OF THE
RENEGADE LYRIC WRITER

ONCE there was a lyric writer named Mr. Amazon,
And being a lyric writer he spent most of his days
          with his pajamas on.
He loved people until they got interested in song
          writing and asked him, which comes first,
                    the lyrics or the music,
And then he was less enthusic,
And also since he wrote words for the music in
          musical comedies
Why he noted a great similarity between singers
          and the man-eating horses of Diomedes,
Because although the singers couldn't eat the
          tunes, you could always recognize the tunes
                    as Chopin's or Rodgers' or Schumann's,
Well, they ate his lyrics the way the man-eating
          horses of Diomedes ate humans.
He was always complaining that Gee whiz,
Some people had to swallow their own words,
          but singers only swallowed his,
And he swore that if he ever met a female
          singer who would pronounce his words he
          would offer her his heart and hand and
                    undying loyalty
And 12½ per cent of his royalty.
Then one day he heard a new female singer in
          rehearsal
And his feelings underwent a reversal.
Her enunciation was fabulous,
He heard every one of his rhymes, even
                    the most polysyllabulous,
So to show his admiration and confidence he wrote

a new song especially for her, beginning The
Leith police releaseth us, releaseth us the
    police of Leith,
And on opening night he sent her a perfect
    rose, but it seems she was a Spaniard
    and she sang the song with the rose
        between her teeth.
Mr. Amazon couldn't even distinguish a vowel,
It was like hearing a lama with a loose tooth
    talking to a barber through a hot towel.
Mr. Amazon no longer writes lyrics, he writes
    radio commercials, because there is one
    fact on which he finally pounced—
When a writer rhymes "sour stomach" with
    "kidney tubes," it may not be prosody
        but, boy, is it pronounced!

—OGDEN NASH.

GOOD CLEAN FUN

YOU keep your football, baseball, theaters and bridge; when it
comes to recreation, I guess I'm different. I like to wash dishes. I
just love to wash dishes. Show me a sink full of dirty dishes and
I'm happy the rest of the day.

Whenever I am invited to dine at the home of friends, I always
make a proviso that they will let me do the dishes. Of course, I
don't let them know it, but I rarely enjoy the meal, because I am
in such a hurry to get through, so that I can get into the kitchen.

You've heard people say, "Give me plenty of hot water and I
don't mind doing dishes." Huh! Why, I don't care if the water's
hot or cold. Others say they would just as soon wipe if they have
plenty of towels. Not me; give me only one towel, and make it
one of those brand-new ones that slip all over the plates and
don't absorb any water. Now that's my idea of fun. Or else one

of those old linty towels that shed on the glasses. Sometimes I'll stick to one glass for hours trying to get the lint off. Silverware is fun to do, but nothing can compare with greasy pots and pans. I always keep them for last.

Each week I look forward to Wednesday night; that is when I call on the Nelsons. They have two daughters who go to high

school, and they leave so early in the morning that they never have time to do the breakfast dishes. By the time Mrs. Nelson gets up she has to start preparing lunch. After lunch she's too busy to wash dishes, as she must dust and clean and start getting dinner ready. By the time dinner is over, there is a grand pile of dirty dishes in the sink. I always manage to pop in just as they are finishing dinner. They are so sweet to me, they let me wash the whole business . . . yes, and dry them too.

I wish I dared call oftener, but I suppose there is no use taking the chance of spoiling a good thing.

—LIONEL ALLYN.

NOBODY HOME

ON Sundays, when the weather's clear
    And favorable for sport,
Within our yard we post a guard,
    And make our house a fort.
And if at dusk he spies a form
    With basket, creel or dish,
He whistles low, to let us know
That some kind neighbor, all aglow,
    Is bringing gifts of fish.

The Smiths prefer Lake Overstock
    For muskellunge or trout.
The Joneses seek Great Salmon Creek,
    And weekly clean it out.
They never seem to draw a blank,
    Their score is always plus;
Their hauls may run a quarter ton,
And when they've had their fill of fun,
    They always think of us.

They fish for recreation's sake—
   They chant, as though they mean it.
Which means they like to catch a pike,
   But will not stoop to clean it.
At intervals—six weeks or more—
   We tolerate a filet;
But junior whales with armored scales,
Great, staring eyes, and bones like nails!
Even our cat recoils and quails,
   Regarding them as silly.

Is that a whistle? Douse the glim!
   Quick, turn that TV off!
Let every room be like a tomb.
   For heaven's sake, don't cough!
For here they come with forty pounds
   Of clammy flesh and fin.
Be firm, my heart; herewith we start:
Today, for all their anglers' art,
   They shall not catch us in!

                  —C. P. DONNEL, JR.

FAMOUS CRIMES
The Teaspoon Murder

IN the annals of crime, few cases are less interesting than the case of Professor Poppit.

In the year 1846, in the village of Cum-Poodley in the Bog, Middlesex, Professor Poppit, a retired Latin teacher, stepped out of his house to go to the store. That was the last that was seen of him until he got to the store. Once there, he purchased a bag of figs, two pounds of potatoes, cheese, a pound of shag—he was an inveterate smoker—and three clay pipes. Four hours later his body was found in the middle of the main street.

The time of the murder could not be established exactly, though he was known to be alive at a quarter to.

Alastair Quigg, the principal witness, deposed that he had seen the victim carrying his packages, and had inquired if he knew the time. Professor Poppit had replied that he did, set down his packages and fished out an enormous silver watch, which had been presented to him on the occasion of his retirement. This watch possessed no hour hand, it having been broken off accidentally, but it kept remarkable time as to minutes, and Professor Poppit was excessively proud of it. He placed it to his ear, consulted it carefully, replaced it in his weskit pocket, gathered up his packages and remarked that it was a quarter to.

"A quarter to what?" inquired Quigg.

"A quarter to the hour," replied Professor Poppit.

"A quarter to what hour?" asked Quigg.

"A quarter to," said Poppit, and moved off.

Medical examination disclosed that Professor Poppit had been struck repeatedly on the head with a small silver object, probably a teaspoon. He had seemed to be in the best of health, and apparently had no reason to beat himself on the head with a teaspoon.

To add to the mystery, his watch was found a short distance from the body, all dented. It had stopped at ten to, thus fixing the time of the murder at ten to something.

This proved to be of no great help, and another unsolved murder took its place in the long list of Famous Crimes.

—JOHN BAILEY.

I NEVER HAD A LESSON IN MY LIFE

I SHALL never, I fear,
Have a concert career,
   And my talents will all go for naught;
But it's really a crime
That I don't have the time
   To have myself properly taught.

I don't wish to seem queer,
But my musical ear
   Is admitted to be quite unique;

If a violin's flat
I can tell where it's at——
   It's a musical gift, so to speak.

I had barely been born
When I picked up a horn
   And played Elmer, Where Art Thou? by Strauss;
As the notes died away,
I can truthfully say
   There was not a dry eye in the house.

As a mere child of three
I could give you high C
   Just by sticking a pin in my brother;
By the time I was six
I was beating with sticks
   On a pan that belonged to my mother.

There were some simple tunes
I could play on balloons,
   Such as Warum and La Traviata;
I could run up the scales
Just by picking my nails,
   And I often composed a sonata.

You never did see
Such a child prodigy;
   And it seems a great shame, in a way,
That I just sort of dropped it——
If I hadn't stopped it
   I might have been famous today.

                        —JOHN BAILEY.

HOW TO EAT

ALTHOUGH the demands of etiquette, including table manners, seem to have relaxed considerably in recent years, apparently by general consent, some of us feel that we should try to maintain certain standards. Otherwise, we shall have chaos. I have already noticed behavior in public and elsewhere which leads me to believe that Neanderthal Man is not yet extinct.

Surely no one, when dining with a fastidious host and hostess, perhaps old friends who have gone on to the finer things of life since you saw them last, would willingly draw upon himself a look which too plainly means, "Where do you think you are— home?" The following brief refresher course is for those who may wish to avoid such a *contretemps:*

1. When entering the dining room avoid giving an impression of unseemly haste, as though you might start pushing at any moment. A seat has been provided for you in advance, and you will eventually get it. This isn't Musical Chairs.

2. The soup should present no great hazards, especially if this course is omitted, as it sometimes is. So far so good.

3. If cucumbers are served with the fish, it is permissible, though not obligatory, to remark that you like cucumbers, but

they do not like you. Do not go into the subject in greater detail. Not another word. Please!

4. Do not make tentative passes at various pieces of chicken before transferring one of them to your plate, as if you found the silver a little difficult to manage, or something. Everybody knows what you're after.

5. Don't spend too much time chasing an elusive green pea around your plate with your fork. If it seems determined to play hard-to-get for an indefinite period, subdue it with some blunt instrument or give up. It is probably not the last green pea on the market.

6. Corn on the cob is not served at formal dinners. If it were, the dinner would cease to be formal.

7. Don't use the cat-and-mouse technique on your salad. Eat it or don't eat it. It is perfectly *comme il faut,* however, to leave part of it on your plate, on the off-chance that strawberry short-cake may be coming later. There's always hope.

8. Nothing so readily betrays the outsider as inability to distinguish between fork foods and spoon foods. The only instances where a spoon may be employed—well, I'll come back to that if I have time.

9. Never treat cream puffs as a finger food unless you have three generations of money behind you.

10. Don't feel too awful if you had one or two accidents that could hardly have escaped the notice of your host and hostess. After all, you knew them when.

—WILL CUPPY.

RULES FOR CAR PUSHING

HIGH on our list of winter games is the exciting sport of car pushing. Up and down the snowy highways players of this game—their happy faces aglow with thrombosis and hoarfrost—gail shove heavy automobiles and cry out cheerfully to the spectator

"Hey, bud, how about a push?" To which the spectators reply, "Cut your wheels, Mac; cut your wheels!"

Considering its popularity, this game deserves an official set of rules. And here they are, if you will kindly stop grinding that starter and pay attention:

1. Play is between an offensive platoon and a defense man.

2. The defense man—sometimes called the Dope—must remain seated in his car. His object is to outwit the offensive platoon, or pushers, by such means as leaving hand brake on, leaving ignition off, steering into snowdrifts, and so on.

3. An offensive platoon consists of the following positions: right fender, left fender, rear bumper, left-door handle, taillight and flanker. The flanker may not push, but must walk alongside, calling out the plays.

4. Any pusher caught wearing overshoes is to be ruled ineligible.

5. Rear bumper alone is permitted to push with both hands. He may not wear gloves, however.

6. Under very icy conditions, an extra player may be called into the game. This player is known as the traction man. It is the duty of the traction man to ring doorbells along the way and ask for a bucket of ashes. If he gets any, he may throw them under the car wheels, shouting as he does, "There, that oughta do it!" In a neighborhood where everybody has oil burners, however, a traction man is of little or no use.

7. No one but left-door handle is allowed to interfere with the defense man. He may do this by reaching in the driver's window and jiggling the steering wheel.

8. Game is over when pushers retire, leaving defense man and car blocking a main intersection. Or if motor catches, which isn't likely.

9. A shove by another car is considered foul. The penalty for this is 100 points above the line or locked bumpers.

—W. F. MIKSCH.

WHIMSEYISM

A CLOCK is something they have in an office, so you can tell how late you wish you weren't in the morning, what time to go out to lunch before and come back after, and how long before you can start stopping work by stalling along until.

—COLONEL STOOPNAGLE.

SLIDING SCALE

A SALMON remarked to his mate:
"My dear, are you putting on weight?
    You were six and a half
    When you slipped from the gaff,
But they're claiming, right now, you were eight."

—NORMAN R. JAFFRAY.

HYPOCHONDRIA CAN BE FUN

NO, doc, I didn't come here for a diagnosis. I always diagnose my own troubles bright and early, but the catch is how to keep the symptoms hot until the doctor comes.

Just like the other night I went home from work with a high fever: hot and cold all over, palpitations and sense of panic. "Sudden and tempestuous onset," like it says in the books. Probably something in the strep family. But when I get home and sit for fifteen minutes with the thermometer in my mouth, it comes up 97.9. The fevers like I have elude the most delicate clinical thermometers. I got a theory about it I'll tell you sometime. Remember that "cold light" they discovered? I got cold fevers—mighty hard for the ordinary practitioner to spot.

I been having a creeping type of coronary thrombosis for

years, unrecognized by any doctor. And don't think I haven't given you fellows plenty of chance to spot it. When my heart goes bumpety-bump, I hop on the bus to the clinic, but by the time I get there and my chest man can take a look at me, the ticker sounds to him like it was "consistent with normal action."

Sometimes I get spots like licorice jelly beans in front of my eyes. The last doc I told about them said, "Relax! I've had spots in front of my eyes for years. In fact, just last week I was looking through a microscope and gave a positive diagnosis of trichinosis in a guy's blood. Those microbes were swimming around in that specimen like the girls in Billy Rose's Aquacade, and I couldn't figure how the patient had lived that long. The next day I remembered those spots in front of my eyes and we checked again. Those spots were the spit and image of trichinae. Absolutely!"

I said, "Doc, I come here for a check and doublecheck, not to listen to the autobiography of a bum guesser." Shopping around among the medics like I do, you get onto their dodges. Let 'em run into a case of psychosomatic liver and off they go telling about livers they have come in contact with over the years.

Of course, even the layman can make a diagnostic mistake. I remember one day right in my office I got a distinct brain flash, and I figured it for a tumor on the left lobe. Well, before I could get to the phone and call my skull specialist for an appointment, I got that flash again, only this time it looked like it came through the ground-glass partition. So just on a chance, I peeked over the partition, and they had a photographer in there taking flash shots of an old guy who was going to retire the next week and

they wanted his picture for Public Relations. My motto is never take up a doctor's time before I've checked the whole situation.

You can't find a thing, doc? You think I ought to see a psychiatrist? No soap. It's bad enough picking up all these diseases of the bones, joints, inner ear, heart muscle, kidneys, lymphatic system, small capillaries and colon that elude you medical docs. But if I get so I can't flop down on a couch for a nap without analyzing myself, I'll be nuts in a week.

—FOTHERGIL FOSTER.

DER HARE UND DER TURTLER

EIN Hare ben outswellen mit der chester und braggen mit grosser talken und boasten. Der Hare ben geclaimen der record speeden mit gerunnen der racers.

Ein Turtler ben outsticken der noggen und snorten mit der disdainer. Der Turtler iss betten mit oddsers der Hare ben gebeaten in ein racen mit der Turtler.

Der racen ben gestarten und das Hare ben obercrossen der finisher marken mit grosser rushen. Der Hare ben gewinnen der racen sooner das Turtler ben upstarten. Der Turtler iss ein Donderhead.

—DAVE MORRAH.

WHIMSEYISM

A slice of bread is fine for making a sandwich with two of them, and beef.

—COLONEL STOOPNAGLE.

CRUSTIFFER COLIMBUS AND THE AMUVVERY OF DISKERRICA

MANY gears a-yoa, Queen Spainabella of Izz heard a night slock at the core of her dassle. There stood a young jen from Manno-a, Italy, who gowed bracefully and egged a bawdience with Her Hyal Royness. This bawdience the Queen gillingly wave.

"I would leerly duvv to wail sestword and amuvver Diskerrica, oh, Seen," he quedd. "But I am dort of shoa. My booket-emp is pockty. Would you kingtact the Con and see if you can mare up a bit of skunny? If you would, I'd be happy to fit splifty-splifty on anyturn that things up."

The Deen, who was anything but a quoap, immediately recognized the mansairity of the sin, plus the proffability of possit in the deal. So she somehow got akold of the Hing, and they mound the fazooma, buying Colimbus bee small throats—the Peena, the Ninta and the Manta Saree-a. This made Holumbus excruciatingly cappy, and, quanking the Theen on nended bee, he forthwith set mare for Assailica, the tune of opperlandity. And it was lunths maiter, on Octwelver toabth, horteen fundred and tooty-nine, that our hung yeero eventually landed on the shessolit doors of the Bahamas, after hardy menships and poissa-dintments. This afeazing mate changed the hiss of corstery, and with it American startery histed.

—COLONEL STOOPNAGLE.

LETTER FROM A FAIRLY UNKNOWN WOMAN

LAST year when Mary Ann was eleven she wrote shy, rambling letters from camp, begging for comic books and potato chips. This year it is different. I shall not gild the lily, but rather present the evidence as it was presented to me:

Dear Mummy: I like the second year here at Mishigoa better than the first. There is a girl in our cabin who takes toe dancing and is going to go to Hollywood. She says she does not want to wash dishes all her life like her mother.

Another girl is Jennie K. She sleeps over me in a bunk. She leans over and says she is taking piano lessons because she wants to go to Carnegie Hall and not stay home when she is old and beat rugs.

I gess you know Connie H. Last Year I didn't like her at all because she was such a show-off thinking she was an actress. But she says she is going to Broadway after Junior High and not turn out something with a red face over an oven like someone she knows at home.

All the girls who are close to me are like these.

Last week we had a treasure hunt and we walked miles and couldn't find a single clue. Miss Frishwacker gave us the treasure anyway. She felt sorry for us. I don't blame her. The treasure was potato chips and you know about my diet.

On the hunt I met June Frobishham who goes to painting school and is going to be a great artist in a few years. She says she decided on some kind of a thing like that after watching her mother drag out the electric washing machine every Monday and nearly die hanging the stuff up and wringing and rinsing.

She says girls go through an awful lot if they don't look out.

Sunday is visitors day for parents and please bring wave lotion, curl pins; one of your old but good dresses, the kind you say, oh, this old thing, but is really only wore a few times; the lone of some high heels; something big and flat I can walk around with on my head and if you won't be too sore, just a little lipstick pomade.

Also that book you gave me for Christmas about If You Want to be a Model. I guess it was Dorothy gave it to me. I don't think you would.

How's Daddy?

Love,

MARYYANNA

P.S.: I have made my name a little fancy as it makes it easier when you have a career.

P.P.S.: Don't throw away my dolls yet. I will keep them for memories.

M.

—ROBERT FONTAINE.

CAFETERIA RULES

NEWS that the following rules for eating in cafeterias are being considered is cheering:

1—Patrons are not to shove people into the salads in detouring this department to begin at the meats.

2—Weaving in and out to acquire articles is not permitted.

3—Do not hide butter under your bread.

4—Nibbling along the way is permissible provided it is confined to articles already placed on your own tray.

5—Tossing rolls and other things to forgetful parties is forbidden.

6—If you want to borrow the catchup or something from another table, ask the party there if he can spare it. Avoid loud argument.

7—When sharing a table with a stranger, do not persist in conversing if he appears uninterested.

8—Desserts are not to be eaten in the telephone booth.

9—When there is a crowd, depart promptly after finishing your meal.

10—Do not stand in the revolving door waiting for the rain to let up.

—CARL BUCHELE.

HOE ME DOWN WITH A DOCEY-DOE

HONOR your partners, balance and whirl,
A right-and-left grand with an elbow twirl;
And here comes the city gal six bars late,
Wrong way round, at a Conga gait.
Oh, they chased pore Bossie from the big red barn;
They lassooed a fiddler quick as Billy-be-darn;
Now it's everybody swing, and allemande ho!
Down the rattlesnake's hole with a docey-doe!

Oh, dance with the dolly with the hole in her stockin',
Though her brakes keep lockin' while her engine's knockin'.
Oh, dance with the dolly with the hole in her head.
Drop the gent a curtsy. Yah, drop dead!
Spin that little dear through a seesaw reel.
Drag her round back by the blister on her heel.
Ain't this fun, Granny? No, chile, no.
Whoever called this dancin' was a Cotton-Eyed Joe.

City gal can't tell a left-hand mill
From a swift right cross, and she never will.
So poke her with your spurs, boys, boot her through the air,
Ketch her on the fly by the braid in her hair.
Sling her by the ears till she flaps like thunder!
Sashay to the horse trough and hold her noggin under.
Hurry up, fireman, don't be slow.
Where's the inhalator? Where's the Old Crow?

Oh, one yank her this-a-way, t'other yank that.
When she comes apart, gents, all fall flat,
Then wring out that dishrag and chassé four.
Go chassé yourself out the old side door.

Birdie in a cage keeps turnin' mighty green!
Who spiked the applejack with Benzedrine?
Oh, some bring a shovel and some bring a hoe
And bury me, boys, where the locoweeds grow.

City gal's got such spindly legs.
Her ribs bash easy as banty eggs.
Pop! go her buttons and her eyeballs. Yipe!
City gal shore is the puny type;
All bogged down like the old mess wagon,
Hind wheel broke and her petticoat draggin',
Slap-silly, staggerin' to and fro
In a bolt and a half of calico.
Keno! And home, gents, heel-and-toe,
While Mayhem p'menades with Vertigo!

—ETHEL JACOBSON.

ADDRESS BOOK

THE only friends who move, I think,
Are those whose names are down in ink!

—BETTY ISLER.

FAMOUS CRIMES
The Woxley Affair

EARLY in November, 1894, a small but distinguished company had gathered in the great drawing room of Woxley Hall to await the dinner gong. Present were the host and hostess, Lord and Lady Woxley; Sir Henry Lemmings; the Duke and Duchess of Wartly; and Alfred Matham, the critic. It was the latter whom tragedy was to strike, ironically, like a dinner gong.

For some minutes he had been brooding over the possibility that roast lamb, which he did not care for, would be served. Finally he could stand the suspense no longer.

"I say, Charles," he burst out, "I sincerely trust we are not having roast lamb. You know how strongly I feel about roast lamb. Or, indeed, lamb in any form."

"Quite. You may set your fears at rest. I believe we are having a roast of beef." He turned to Lady Woxley. "Isn't that true, my dear?"

"We are if it got here. We ordered one, but it may not have got here. If not, we're having a ragout."

"Ragu," said Alfred Matham absently. "The 't' is silent."

"Oh. Well, that's what we're having if the roast didn't get here."

"I certainly hope it got here," said Lord Woxley. "I love roast beef."

" 'Like,' " said Matham. "You can't 'love' roast beef. You 'like' it."

"Quite so," said Woxley.

"And you should say you 'trust' it got here. 'Hope' refers to the future, so you can't say you 'hope' it got here."

"Roast beef doesn't agree with me," said the duchess, tapping Matham playfully across the nose with her fan. "I always take three teaspoonsful of baking soda afterward."

" 'Teaspoonfuls,' I think you'll find you mean," said Matham, rubbing his nose. " 'Three teaspoonsful' means three separate and distinct spoons. Haw!"

" 'Spoonsful,' I always thought," said Sir Henry. "Each of the spoons were filled three times, and that makes three spoonsful."

"Each of the spoons 'was' filled three times," said Matham. "However, the point is easily settled. I will go to the library and consult the Oxford Unabridged Dictionary."

He went off.

A moment later, Sir Henry rose and announced that he was going to wash up.

Matham had not returned when the dinner gong sounded and, after a search, his body was discovered in the library. Medical examination disclosed that he had been beaten to death with the Oxford Unabridged Dictionary. Suspicion directed itself to the other members of the party. However, close questioning by police failed to reveal any motive for the crime.

Sir Henry advanced the theory that in getting the dictionary down from the shelf, Matham had slipped and the heavy book had fallen on his head, killing him instantly.

No further clues were discovered, however, and Matham's death, whether accident or murder, remains to this day one of the most mysterious of the Famous Crimes.

—JOHN BAILEY.

THE BLISSFUL DREAM OF MR. FARR

Once, there was a man named Mr. Farr,
And he dreamed he had a wife who, summer or
      winter, didn't make him close the window
      when she got in the car.
If he inadvertently ran through a red light, she
      made no remark,
And she never told him where and how to park.
When he was sad she was silent, and when he was
      cheery she was cheerier,
And if the Smiths drove to the seashore in two
      hours via Route 212, and he insisted on
      Route 176 and took three hours, she found
      Route 176 infinitely superior.
When he came home in the rain, she had a hot
      bath drawn for his arrival,
And if she wanted to see the new Boyer picture
      and he wanted the old Marx Brothers'
      picture, they saw the revival.
Although she didn't smoke, she had ash trays
      everywhere, but if he dropped ashes on the
      floor, she wasn't critical or heckly,
And during baseball broadcasts she didn't talk,
      she kept score, and correckly.
She provided him with unscented soap,
And greeted his feeblest jest like a studio audience
      greeting a mention of Hope by Crosby or
      Crosby by Hope.
You understand that Mr. Farr was a bachelor,
And to a bachelor such dreams come nachelor.
                        —OGDEN NASH.

MRS. SPOONER'S METHOD OF TURVING
A CARKEY FOR DANKSGIVING THINNER

YOU turve a carkey just like you'd butt up any other curd, spactically preaking, except that a lurkey is often targer.

First, fize and race the dungry highners. Then, assuming the opper prattitude, remove your vote and kest and sloal up your reaves.

Tace the cooked plurkey dack-side bown on the pilver slatter. Fabb the carving groark hermly in the left fand and habb it into the jerkey up to the tilt, with the brines of the fork on either side of the test-bone. (If you're heft-landed, simply proverse the receedure.) Now take the narving kife in the right hand and scutt through the kin between the begs and the loddy. Lay the fife and nork down, nacing your bree against the nessy if turkessary —although this is a mitt bessy—reloove the megs and disbodd them from the jointy. Then wutt off the kings. Separate the jeckund soints from the stumdricks. Carve the mest breet into thin, slosswise cryces. On either back of the side-bone, you'll find two choice oices of dark meat called peesters, which are very tiddy daintbits indeed. If you're a sighful trellfish, as most arvers car, you'll direct the other tenners' a-dine-shun elsewhere while you shove these morshus lussels surreptitiously into your own tate pu-mash-toes.

For a fall smamily, turve only one side of the carkey, using what's left for kurkey à la Ting, tetry Turkazzini and hacky tursh. The bones, of course, make fine surkey toop, but after that, there's memming but the nuthery.

—COLONEL STOOPNAGLE.

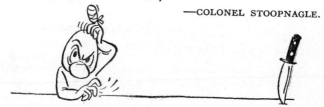

EXTRA! MYSTERY SOLVED

NOW it can be told! Through an exclusive interview with a captured German field marshal, Heinrich Rausvonhaus Von und Zu Schnitzel, the mystery of the disappearance of Adolf Hitler has been solved.

The heretofore unpublished statement by General Rausvonhaus and so forth, follows untranslated:

"Ich ben ein locomotiver proceeden mit breaknecken speeden. Ein automobilser also ben gecomen mit breaknecken speeden. Das locomotiver ben gemaken ein huffen-puffen und stacken-smoken! Das automobilser ben gemaken der grosser motor roaren!

"Ober das graden crossen ben gestanden der Führer—Heil Hitler! Der Führer iss geraisen der handsers mit 'Halten!' und 'Stoppen!'

"Das locomotiver outgaben mit ein rooten-tooten und dingerlingen! Der automobilser gesounden ein grosser honken und braken screechen.

"Ich ben gecomen ein exploden mit der grosser crashen mit donder und blitzen! Ach! Der Führer—Heil Hitler!—iss gemincer meaten."

—DAVE MORRAH.

UNTITLED MS.

MR. NELSON TRAVIS,
GOLD SEAL PUBLISHING HOUSE,
NEW YORK, N. Y.

Dear Nels: Glad you like my new novel and I'm happy to have Gold Seal bring it out. I'm not too sold on the title "And Then

Thou," so I'm sure we can get together on a little thing like that. What do you suggest?

Cordially,
(signed) Dick
E. Richard Daingerfield.

Mr. E. Richard Daingerfield,
Lakeside, Connecticut.

Dear Dick: As you say, the title is no issue. I rather like "The Front Room," since there is a reference to a front room on Page 219 of the manuscript: ". . . Watson had painted the front room first, and then moved on through the house painting each room. . . ." So far as possible, I always like the title to tie in with the story.

Sincerely,
Nels.

NELSON TRAVIS
GOLD SEAL PUBLISHING HOUSE
NEW YORK, N. Y.
GOT GOOD LAUGH OUT OF TITLE WHICH OF COURSE WAS A GAG. WHAT'S THE MATTER WITH "AND THEN THOU?"   RICHARD

Mr. E. Richard Daingerfield,
Lakeside, Connecticut.

Dear Richard: Frankly, I can't see "And Then Thou." What does it mean? I've reread the manuscript carefully, and on Page 378 *there is another reference to a front room:* ". . . Sometimes Watson slept in the back room and sometimes in the front room. . . ." I don't see how you can avoid "The Front Room" as a title.

Sincerely,
Nelson.

Mr. Nelson Travis,
Gold Seal Publishing House,
New York, N. Y.

Dear Nelson: Happened to show a carbon copy of the novel to a friend of mine at Acme Press, and he thought a name like "The Front Room" would be tragic. He even suggested I return the "ten-thousand-dollar" advance and let Acme publish the book under the title "And Then Thou." I didn't tell him the advance was $1000.

> Yours truly,
> E. Richard Daingerfield.

E. RICHARD DAINGERFIELD
LAKESIDE, CONN.
JUST TRYING TO HELP YOU. WHAT'S A PUBLISHER GOOD FOR?
> NELS

NELSON TRAVIS
GOLD SEAL PUBLISHING HOUSE
NEW YORK, N. Y.
LIVE BAIT.   DAINGERFIELD

Mr. E. Richard Daingerfield,
Lakeside, Connecticut.

Dear Mr. Daingerfield: In reference to your untitled manuscript, I must suggest it either be called "The Front Room" or else you had better take it to some other publishing house. I have seen some of the pamphlets printed by Acme Press, and I feel sure that they could do the kind of job you have in mind.

> Yours truly,
> Nelson Travis.

NELSON TRAVIS
GOLD SEAL PUBLISHING HOUSE
NEW YORK, N. Y.
JUST REREAD MS. HOW ABOUT "THE BACK ROOM"?   DICK

E. RICHARD DAINGERFIELD
LAKESIDE, CONN.
TERRIFIC! ABSOLUTELY TERRIFIC! DUST JACKET POSSIBILITIES
UNLIMITED. HOW DID YOU HAPPEN TO THINK OF IT?   NELS

MR. NELSON TRAVIS,
GOLD SEAL PUBLISHING HOUSE,
NEW YORK, N. Y.

Dear Nels: I'm rather proud of it too. You ask how I happened to think of it. Well, on Page 378 it says: ". . . Sometimes Watson slept in the back room and sometimes in the front room. . . ." All of a sudden it hit me—"The Back Room"! But you shouldn't be surprised. After all, don't forget I'm a writer, and I'm supposed to have some imagination.   DICK.

—CASKIE STINNETT.

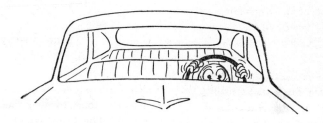

GRIN AND BEAR LEFT

I DON'T want to be classed among the pedantics,
But next time I visit friends who have moved to
      the country I want to get together with them
      on terminology, or semantics.
When you ask them on the telephone how to get
      there they smilingly cry that it is simple,
In fact you can practically see them dimple—

You just drive on Route 402 to Hartley and then
    bear left a couple of miles till you cross a
    stream,
Which they imply is alive with tench, chub, dace,
    ide, sturgeon and bream,
And you go on till you reach the fourth road on the
    right,
And you can't miss their house because it is on a
    rise and it is white.
Well, it's a neighborhood of which you have never
    been a frequenter,
But you start out on 402 and soon find yourself
    trying to disentangle Hartley from East
    Hartley, West Hartley, North and South
    Hartley and Hartley Center,
And you bear left a couple of miles, peering through
    the windshield, which is smattered with gnats
    and midges,
And suddenly the road is alive with bridges,
And your tires begin to scream
As you try to decide which bridge spans a rill, which
    a run, which a branch, which a creek, which
    a brook or river, and which presumably a
    stream.
And having passed this test, you begin to count
    roads on the right, than which no more ex-
    hausting test is to be found,
For who is to say which is a road, which a lane,
    which a driveway and which just a place where
    somebody backed in to turn around?
But anyhow, turning around seems a good idea, so
    there is one thing I don't know still:
Whether that white house where the cocktails are
    getting warm and the dinner cold is on a ridge,
    a ledge, a knoll, a rise or a hill.

                        —OGDEN NASH.

YOU'VE GOT TO EAT SOMEWHERE

"HELLO. Haskins Building Company? I'd like to speak with Mr. Arnold Haskins, please. . . . Hello. Mr. Haskins? . . . Good day to you, sir! How's the construction business this very fine morning? . . . Oh, no (ha-ha) this isn't Mr. Burtt, of Mammoth Insurance. This is Horace Dunkett. Remember me? Sure is a long time back to those days at Riverdale Commercial when I went around with your sister. How is she, by the way? . . . Good! Great! Glad to hear it.

"Well, I'll get right to the point, Arnold. You've heard a lot about the Karokian Club, of course, and its youth work, and you know many of our members personally. We'd like very much, Arnold, to have you with us as a fellow Karokian. I happen to be membership chairman, and the boys were saying only last week Arnold Haskins is the type of new member we want—a fine, responsible, progressive citizen. That's exactly what they said.

"In fact, the boys—— I beg your pardon? You say you have every evening filled up? Of course I realized you must have, because you are a busy man. That's just the kind of member we want. It's the busy men who get things done. I always say give the job to the busiest man; he'll get it done. You see, we don't meet in the evenings anyway; we meet at suppertime. You've got to eat somewhere, so why not eat with us?

"You are in favor of promoting healthy youth, the citizens of tomorrow, aren't you? . . . That's right, Arnold, of course you are. You're a Karokian in spirit already. As a matter of fact, Arnold, you only get out of life what you put into it, and we feel that the Karokian Club can do something for you. It will take you out of the daily business routine into a totally different atmosphere—relaxation and recreation with a great bunch of fellows, and interesting speakers, and only an hour or so every week. You will give it a try, won't you? . . .

"What's that? You say perhaps next year? Come on, Arnold, old man; if you like Karokianism next year, you'll like it this year. Don't put off till tomorrow—— I tell you what. How about just coming to the next meeting as my personal guest? . . . That's the spirit, Arnold; I knew you wouldn't let us down!

"Just by coincidence we're having a supper meeting at the hotel tonight, so we'll be seeing you, eh? By the way, we've got you down for chairman of the construction committee. You've read in the papers about the boys' lodges we're going to build at Lake Nepisiwaaksis. Well, you'll have charge of the whole project —that's the kind of confidence we have in you. In fact, you'll be able to get right down to work on details with the architect after supper. See you at 6:30, Arnie boy."

—STUART TRUEMAN.

LIVING MADE DIFFICULT

THE concept of the average American family being steadily portrayed in television commercials is producing in this semicaptive viewer a growing sense of frustration.

Each American home is pictured as a snug little harbor festooned with automatic devices, directed by a chic hostess in a Jacques Fath tea apron and a thirty-five-dollar upsweep. The children are semi-automatic little dreamboats operating from a wall plug, who delight in servicing daddy with slippers and pipe as he sinks into his after-dinner coma. This isn't true at our house, as the following script will show.

Grimley Meeps, a lower-bracket taxpayer bearing a tiresome resemblance to the author of these lines, turned the corner and bore down on his residence. Few changes had occurred in the manor house since morning. Several shutters had fallen off, and a young marksman had shattered the porch light with an air gun, but substantially it was the same weather-beaten bailiwick.

As he came in the rear door, his wife Gloria was trepanning a carp at the kitchen sink.

"I'm home," said Grimley. "Any mail?"

"The usual. Three final notices and something marked 'Summons' in Old English lettering. Rather pretty."

Grimley sighed and sat down at the kitchen table. "Where are the children? In jail?"

"They left here with your fishing tackle. I believe they said something about knocking down walnuts." Gloria turned suddenly from the sink. "Grimley, what's the matter with us? We don't live like the people in the television commercials. Why can't we have an automatic marmalade spreader or a bath finished in Gooper Tile? We never take junkets on Diesel-powered trains through scenic wonderlands. We don't have white side-wall tires on the car."

"We don't even have a car," said Grimley listlessly. "It caught fire on the bridge this morning and I had to shove it in the river."

"Well, that's a relief," said Gloria. "Without that thing eating its head off in repair bills maybe we can afford some new sheets." She paused. "Why are you staring at me, Grimley?"

"You haven't said a word about the insurance money."

"Insurance money! You mean to say you had that heap insured?"

"Certainly. The only smart thing I did was listen to my Spellbound Mutual man. They pay triple indemnity if the fire occurs in the middle of a river. The check will be here in the morning."

"Darling," cooed Gloria, "I always knew you'd make good." She changed rapidly into a tea apron and pushed her hair into the semblance of an upsweep. "As soon as the children get home they're going to carry slippers and pipes until they're blue in the face. After dinner, you and I will curl up in front of the television set and take notes. We'll show those people how really to live."

—DICK ASHBAUGH.

SEMI-SCIENTIFIC FACTS

THE gases in a comet's tail
Would cause us all to turn quite pale.

Some electrons are so small
We wonder if they're there at all.

In forty-nine thousand and sixty, B.C.,
A caveman named Oogoo was stung by a bee.

The largest giant that ever grew
Liked folks so well he ate a few.

—JOHN BAILEY.

NEW LIGHT ON DINOSAURS

EVERYWHERE you go these days you hear people asking, "What happened to the dinosaurs?"

In view of the fact that they disappeared 300,000,000 years ago, scientists have recently abandoned the theory—advanced by Professor Queppens—that they would come around soon enough when they got hungry.

Now this little play does not pretend to answer that scientific riddle, but we do hope it will bring people closer to the dinosaurs and give us a better understanding of their problem. Their problem, of course, is that they're extinct.

[*The scene is a sort of mudhole with a lot of fern trees around it. All the dinosaurs have disappeared except two—whom, for convenience, we'll call* GEORGE *and* FRANK.]

GEORGE: Say, where is everybody?

FRANK: Hello, George. Howza boy?

G: Pretty good. I stubbed my toe on a boulder this morning. I imagine it is going to hurt something fierce when the message reaches my small brain.

F: Wouldn't be surprised. You ought to take a couple pounds of aspirin.

G: What's aspirin?

F: I don't know. Say, I weighed myself this morning, and do you know what?

G: No, what?

F: I've lost four tons.

G: You don't say so. Were you too heavy?

F: Yes. Now I'm just forty tons. I *feel* better.

G: You're a good color too.

F: What color am I?

G: I don't know. Say, what are you doing this afternoon?

F: Nothing. I'd sort of like to listen to the ball game, but I haven't got a radio.

G: Neither have I.

F: And there's no ball game.

G: No.

F: It certainly gets me where everybody is.

G: Me too.

F: Let's go hunt for them, shall we?

G: All right. You go that way and I'll go this way.

[*They disappear.*]

—JOHN BAILEY.

THE JOLLY PAINTERS

THE painting crew which is daubing up the moldy mansion I recently picked up for something slightly short of a king's ransom consists of two happy characters named Rolph and Lyman and their sensitive and artistic boss, Adolph Lamur.

It had been my impression that the painters would arrive, follow my instructions, complete the job and be gone, leaving only spots on the windows and green footprints in the bathtub. Not at all.

Adolph showed me samples which I tentatively examined. As I seemed to pick one or the other, Adolph would indicate, by placing his hand on his hip and wincing, or groaning slightly, that my choice was impossible. Then he showed me what I was going to have.

Having disposed of me, Adolph disappeared—I presume to tell other people what colors they should have. Two sensitive fellows in white suits, Rolph and Lyman, now arrived. The first day it was too dark for them to paint. The second day, too cold. The third day they got up on a staging and went after the ceiling, working from opposite sides of the room toward each other, crossing over with a deft jump, as in a circus, apologizing and

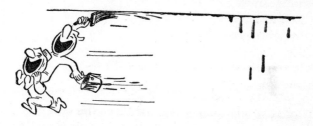

bowing when they sprinkled paint on each other and continuously singing mournful folk songs about the pale dead girl in the valley or the sad old woman in the hills.

If I complained of the noise or examined the paint, they jumped down and spent four hours at three dollars an hour explaining how sensitive they were and how anyone watching them was very distracting.

When I complained to Adolph, he said flatly, "Please do not irritate my men. Homeowners we can find all over, but painters are scarce!"

O.K., but next time my house is painted I'll do it myself, even if I have to wear a diving suit to protect me from the paint and hire a lawyer to protect me from my own choice of colors. I'm sensitive too. And I don't get paid for it.

—ROBERT FONTAINE.

FATHERS, ARISE!

AN organization I would go through fire and water for—preferably both at the same time—is the Activated Fathers of America. This is a nonprofit group with offices in abandoned stone quarries throughout most of the principal cities. We meet monthly and discuss ways to outsmart children.

The main topic at our last meeting was Use of the Loch Ness Monster in Getting Children to Bed. The majority voted for corporal action at bedtime, offset by some sort of stewed fruit in the child's diet during the day.

At our next meeting we will discuss eating habits of children. We are preparing papers on such subjects as Forced Feeding of Crusts, and Vegetable Spurning and What to Do. I have been making carefully detailed notes on my own children and here are some of the findings:

Molly, the ten-year-old, does not like apple, celery or nuts in her apple-celery-nut salad. She will eat it, however, if you substitute tomato surprise, using peach ice cream instead of tomatoes. She refuses head lettuce altogether, claiming she once ate some and got *D* in arithmetic. Carrot strips fascinate her and she likes raw cabbage, but put them together in a salad and she threatens to go live with grandma.

Melinda, a well-preserved child of five, won't eat the outside of anything. She bites a small opening in a piece of toast and then works outward, humming to herself. Within a reasonable distance of the crust she quits cold. When she has enough crusts to circle her plate, she gets down and goes away to play paper dolls. The crusts are removed by the city.

Both of the children will eat any kind of meat as long as it is hamburger on a bun. They like it served with a slice of onion, so they can say, "We didn't want onion on our hamburgers; we wanted mustard." If daddy has just returned from the grocery with a barrel of mustard on his back, they want ketchup. The ketchup bottle is empty, and don't think they hadn't planned it that way.

They like to eat from exotic containers. If you could serve vegetable soup in tiny birchbark canoes, they would eat every drop. An omelet in a flower vase or an umbrella full of milk would put roses in their cheeks.

My report isn't complete, but it will have to wait. Yesterday I looked at the grocery bill, and I am now offering a reward for the top of my head. It went straight up and then blew off in a southwesterly direction.

—DICK ASHBAUGH.

WHIMSEYISMS

IF you will pulverize your used electric-light bulbs, they make one of the best things known for not scattering on your driveway.

A pig cannot write when he has no oink in his pen.

If the equator were just a bit shorter, it wouldn't quite reach around the earth.

—COLONEL STOOPNAGLE.

NOGOLICHE

MODERN art, confusing enough before, is now even worse. It has produced a new master—Nogoliche. Born in 1912, the ninth son of a human hair hair-net net-maker, he was apprenticed at an early age to a Good Humor man, where he became fascinated by the different colors in the ice cream.

"The rich, warm brown of the chocolate covering," he writes, "contrasted by the brilliant white of the vanilla, after you had taken a bite out of it, was a deeply vibrant personal soul experience."

He decided to become a painter. In the beginning, his career was held up for twelve years by the unfortunate delusion that in order to be a painter he had to have a camel's hair-brush, and during these years he traveled extensively in the Orient looking for one. These years were not entirely wasted, however. The desert impressed itself on his life and work.

"The rich, warm brown of the desert," he writes, "contrasted by the brilliant white of the native burnoose, was a deeply personal vibrant experience of the soul."

From the Orient he went to Paris, and his first canvases were produced there. These were the simple expressions of himself, and consisted of a single thin brown line, drawn from left to right across the gleaming white expanse of canvas. In these, one felt the emptiness, the vastness, the space that was in Nogoliche's head.

As M. Severinaux, the French art critic, says, in speaking of these early paintings: "Zee rich, warm brown of zee line, contrasted wiz zee brilliant white of zee canvas, personally geeves deep vibrations of zee soul."

In 1936, Nogoliche came to America, and his later canvases show the result of intense research. No longer content with a simple horizontal line, he began to draw them every which way, and he now has canvases with brown lines on them in almost every direction.

Much has been written, lately, by American art critics, about these canvases, but Nogoliche remains unaffected. He continues to paint anyhow.

He was inspired recently when he spilled some gravy down his white shirt front. "The rich, warm brown of the gravy," he says, "contrasted . . ."

—JOHN BAILEY.

CRIME RAVE

I FAILED to solve this latest crime,
　　So well the author hid it.
I threw the obvious suspect out;
　　And the son-of-a-gun—he did it!

—FRANK R. CANNING.

SHOPWORN

IT was in the middle of the afternoon when my wife telephoned me at the office and said, "Look, we're having company tonight. Aunt Sophie is coming for dinner."

"So what about it?"

"I want you to get something."

I quivered. "Now, listen, dear. Please don't ask me to do any more shopping for you. You know I always mess it up somehow, and get the wrong thing."

"Oh," she said, "you can't possibly mess anything up this time. It's too simple. Even you know enough to get a loaf of bread. We don't need anything else. Just one loaf of bread. Get it?"

"O.K. All right, I'll bring it."

I took an envelope out of my breast pocket and plainly marked on it: "Loaf bread."

At 5:15 I was in Kennedy's bakery.

"One loaf of bread, please."

"What kind?"

What kind? Murder, I had forgotten to ask my wife what kind! I handed the girl a quarter. "Give me five nickels, please, and I'll find out." From past experience, I knew how involved these simple things inevitably become.

There was a phone on the wall, and I put a coin into the box and dialed my number.

"Jule," I said, "what kind of bread do you want?"

"Why, you know we always use whole wheat."

"That's right. I forgot. Thanks."

I hung up the receiver and went back to the counter.

"Whole wheat." I smiled at the girl.

"Hearth or wrapped?"

I sighed. "Wait a minute. I'll find out."

I dialed the phone again. "Jule, I forgot to ask you, do you want the hearth bread or the wrapped?"

She tsk-tsked. "Don't you know we always use the wrapped bread? It's more sanitary."

"That's right. Thanks."

I hung up and went back to the counter.

"Whole wheat, wrapped," I said.

"Enriched or plain?"

My heart sank. I was afraid to make a guess at it—and probably get the wrong thing. I went back to the phone.

"Jule," I asked, "do you want it enriched or plain?"

"Enriched, of course!" she snapped at me. "You should know we've been using the enriched for five years!"

"Oh, certainly. I happened to forget."

I shuffled back to the counter.

"Whole wheat," I said sweetly, "wrapped, enriched."

"Do you want it sliced?"

Rage filled my heart. What did this strange woman mean by cross-examining me so relentlessly? I scowled at her. "Wait a minute," I growled; "I'll find out."

I dialed the phone. "Listen, Jule, I hate to bother you again, but I have to know if you want this loaf sliced or not."

"Oh," she said, "I'm so glad you called again. Aunt Sophie just telephoned me that she won't be able to come to dinner, after all. And we don't need that loaf now."

Joy flooded me. "Hooray!" I shouted as I threw the receiver back on the hook. For once I had shopped to suit my wife!

I turned toward the counter. "Never mind!" I thundered at the girl. "You can keep your old bread!"

And I rushed out of the bakeshop like mad.

—W. E. FARBSTEIN.

RUN FOR THE HILLS—THEY'RE BACK

LATE summer sees the return of Vacationistus Americana (American Vacationists). They are found predominantly sitting in other people's living rooms, sipping cool drinks. Here are some examples of the most widespread types in this group:

The Human Calendar: "We got up to Lake Oleofoleokingaga on the third—no, it wasn't the third; by golly, it was the fourth. The reason I say it was the fourth is that we stopped for gasoline near the lake, and the attendant, who lives there all year around, you know, wiped his brown brow and said, 'Hot fourth, eh?' Wait a minute! By golly, I think it was the third, now that you mention it, because we didn't buy any gas on that day. But that doesn't have anything to do with the story anyway. Anyway, we got up to the lake and——"

The Human Thermometer: "What weather we had! It was ideal. I-d-e-a-l! It was 97.2 degrees here when we left. No sooner did we get out of the city when the temperature dropped to 82.2 degrees. You know, it's at least fifteen degrees cooler in the suburbs. It really got hot up there during the day, though. Went up

to 101.3 last Thursday. But as hot as it was during the day, it was never over 57.1 degrees at night. Had to sleep under two blankets. I figured it all out on paper. The average temperature for the two weeks, including day and night temperatures, would have been 74.4 degrees, but a storm sprang up on the last day and lowered the average to 73.9 degrees."

The Human Camera: "Boy what a place that Riordanville is. I was using a Sesco inverter with a triple-locking spectroscope. It has that flit-filter lens with the undercontact prisms. Well, I posed Madge next to a cranberry bog and got set up. The light meter read .00000002. I checked my exact distance on the Ransco self-bisecting quadrangle and synchronized it with the radioscilloscopic arc-finder. Then I measured the angle of the sun with the binomial sextant and——"

The Human Road Map: "Brother, we certainly had quite a ride from Phenway to Raxville. That's on Route 668B, you know. We got up to Phenway, all right—482.3 miles to be exact. Nice road all the way. Matter of fact, we didn't see one single solitary car on Route 91 from Lasco to Stacy, distance of 47.5 miles if you take the Route 128A cutoff, you know. But from Phenway to Raxville, that was the pay-off. You know Phenway is roughly about 373.28 miles from Raxville on Route 304R and——"

—ROBERT ROWE.

A FOOT ABOUT BITBALL

FOOTBALL is a very spuff roart, and it takes men with lurdy stegs, massel finds and gots of lutz. It sometimes results in noaken broazes and harley chorses and often leaves the player in a kate of temporary stoama, necessitating his being ferried from the streeld on a ketcher. Therefore such thulky bings—and I'm not crozbing about Speakby—as poalder-shads and other peritective prophernalia are required to bresson the number of loozes and keep minns at a bumpimum.

The plame is gayed on a grid called a field-iron and the rawl, instead of being bound like a boap-subble, is shoavel-aipt, like an eggin's rob, so it will kounce bock-eyed and plool the fayers.

When the whifferee's wrestle blows, the stay plarts, and when it blows again, stay plops. The whole idea is for one team to make a skigger boar than the other, and the one with the pewest loints foozes.

If you wish deether furtails, consult the creezident of almost any pollidge, who will happily refer you to the foalen swunds in his athpartic deletment.

The sayers on each plide fine up as lollows:

TEFT LACKLE GEFT LARD SOAVING RENTER GIGHT RARD TIGHT RACKLE
EFT LEND   BORTER-QUACK   IGHT REND
        HEFT LAUGH   HEIGHT RAFF
                    BULL-FACK

P.S.: Oh, yes, and an umferee and two reffpires.

—COLONEL STOOPNAGLE.

ONE PAPER TOWEL

you can get by,
But you can't get dry.

—A. A. LATTIMER.

NOTHING TO IT

THE American home is under attack. A crew of self-styled experts is trying to convert every man into a mechanic-carpenter-electrician-chemist for his own home. These meddlers pour out newspaper columns, magazines and books urging everyone to take home repairs into his own hands. Did you know that drab, outworn curtains can be dyed at home? That you can brighten up your rooms with vivid new colors for a fraction of what new drapes would cost? A few cheap chemicals, easy to obtain, will make these wonderful dyes. Your washtub makes a convenient vat. Your expenses will be:

Ingredients . . . . $	3.50
Stainless-steel mixing spoon	2.00
Total . . . . $	5.50

"You will be astounded at the results," say the experts.

This statement cannot be gainsaid. After one man tried the process, his house looked like a bad day at the I. G. Farben, and the final cost was:

Ingredients . . . . $	3.50
4 stainless-steel mixing spoons (they kept dissolving in the concoction)	8.00
New curtains	52.00
New windows (it apparently dissolves glass too) . . .	44.00
Total . . . . $	107.50

The conversion of common household appliances into new and, to say the least, exotic devices is another popular theme. One zealot puts out a column of helpful hints on wiring, replete with descriptions of electrical marvels and complicated diagrams of circuits—a sort of chummy invitation to arson. The descriptions are long. The circuits are short. Here at last is a chance to get some use out of that waffle iron you were thinking of throwing away. It can be made over into a variable-voltage zwieback grill!

An ordinary transformer, a few cents' worth of wire and a simple relay are all you need. A friend of mine, hungering for a grilled zwieback, tried it. Result: grilled house.

Incidentally, the convince-him-he-has-no-use-for-it-as-it-is approach is a common stratagem. Such insidious phrases as "that outmoded colorvision set you were ready to junk" and "the old 1949 sedan you were going to give away as a Canasta prize" are clichés in this field. If you can believe what you read, the average American ashcan must hold a king's ransom, thanks to this prodigious scrapping. It is not fair to say, however, that all such literature should be suppressed. There are a few expert handy men who pass out really good advice. I happen to be one of the best myself. Here is a tip for which you home owners will thank me:

Billboard Makes Fine Drawbridge

How many times have you wondered what to do with the front door? Don't throw it away! Here is an opportunity to equip your house with the latest refinement in gracious living, a moat-and-drawbridge arrangement for keeping friends away from your television set. An ordinary billboard, such as you can pick up along any highway, makes an ideal drawbridge. A few screws, a length of chain and a simple windlass will do the rest. Your son can assemble it during his recess from kindergarten. The cost is only eighty-six cents, for the hardware.

—TED CARR.

NOTES ON PREHISTORIC MAN

ON all the earth there was no store
For sixty thousand years and more.

The man who first discovered fire
Was dressed in rather odd attire.

The cave man's jaw was bigger than
That of the wife of modern man.

Not a single cave man ever got shot
(Spears were invented, but guns were not).

Quite often the ranks of the cave men got thinner
When a hunter, intending to dine, became dinner.

The cave man's wife had nothing to say;
He'd tap her noggin if she got in the way.

A cave man seldom passed his youth
If he had met Old Sabertooth.

The last time anyone saw Gawk,
He went out for a little walk.

I think I'd give myself a fright
Sitting in a cave at night.

—JOHN BAILEY.

PIANO TUNER, UNTUNE ME THAT TUNE

I REGRET that before people can be reformed, they have
      to be sinners,
And that before you have pianists in the family, you
      have to have beginners.
When it comes to beginners' music,
I am not enthusic.
My opinion of scales
Would not pass through the mails,
And even when listening to something called An
      Evening in My Doll House or The Bee and the
      Clover,
Why, I'd like just once to hear it played all the way
      through, instead of that hard part near the end
      over and over.
Have you noticed about little fingers?
When they hit a sour note, they lingers.
And another thing about little fingers, they are always
      strawberry-jammed or cranberry-jellied-y,
And Chopsticks is their favorite melody,
And if there is one man who I hope his dentist was a
      sadist and all his teeth were brittle ones,

It is he who invented Chopsticks for the little ones.
My good wishes are less than frugal
For him who started the little ones going boogie-woogal,
But for him who started the little ones picking out
  Chopsticks on the ivories,
Well, I wish him a thousand harems of a thousand
  wives apiece, and a thousand little ones by each
  wife, and each little one playing Chopsticks
  twenty-four hours a day in all the nurseries of all
  his harems or wiveries.

—OGDEN NASH.

MRS. SPOONER'S RECIPES
How to Build a Sub Clandwitch

(DEE-THRECKER)

HEE THRUNKS BESH FRED	ONE TYCED SLOMAYTO
GEEDIUM MOB DRAYONNAISE	TREST OF BURKEY, THUTT
MESSING	KIN
STREVERAL SIPS BISP CRAYKON	PAWLT AND SEPPER
THREE BATS OF PUTTER	

BROAST the ted in the e-toastric lekter until it's a bright lown.
Bed sprutter on the hot broasted ted and mett it lelt. On the
burst hunk of fred, med sprayonnaise until it surfers the entire
cuvviss. Now place several slurces of tykey on the second tyce of
sloast, plus a teece or poo of type romayto, and buvver with cay-
kon. Now place the peccund seece a-fop the turst and the third
on seck of the toppund. Now you are ready to consand the soom-
witch. Open your waws jide. If you can't quite grake the maid,
you must be satisfied with two-sander club deckwitches or you
must get a migger bowth.

—COLONEL STOOPNAGLE.

HOW GAY WAS OUR CREDIT

THE two-tone, reversible credit letter, which I hope shortly to offer credit managers in a poisoned wrapper, is the result of puzzled dalliance with a large but coquettish department store. The clearest come-on you ever saw opened this affair—a note from the store, saying that some of the best people found it pleasant to charge things there. The flattering suggestion was clear that I was just the well-heeled, dependable type they liked to have in the store.

Well, inside of two months there came another letter. You wouldn't have known this rude smirch was from the same company. "When we extend credit," said this coldly formal ultimatum—and what a crass name for the relationship hinted in that first scented note—"we expect everything to be paid up at the end of the month. If you cannot do this, call on the sixteenth floor and make other arrangements."

This from the store that had so lately been straightening my tie and fluttering its best sixty-nine-cent handkerchief.

My two-way letter was born right then, and I think credit managers will go for it, as it saves printing up two forms. It can be used either as the beautifully airy Maybasket in which they invite you to come in and rumple the sales manager's hair or as the little snarl a little later which tells you to pay your bill at once. Goes like this:

"Perhaps you are one of the few really nice people who still are not using our handy credit service. We find you have owed us $6 since yesterday. Where is it? If you are not, if you still shop the old-fashioned way, why not try 'Charge-O' sometime, just for a fillip? It's so languorous you'll wonder why you ever bothered carrying bulky old currency which stretches the pockets.

"We have taken the liberty of issuing you one of our pretty charge-account cards, chosen to match your eyes. Just whisper, 'Charge it' to one of the subservient salespersons, and we do the rest. If we do not hear from you promptly on this matter, we will slap a lien on everything you own.

"Many of our customers don't like to soil their fingers writing inky old checks, and they find charging much more diverting.

"If they need cash while downtown, they just borrow ten or twenty from Uncle Walter, our jolly cashier. If you cannot afford to buy here, why don't you get your stuff out of trash barrels? We extend credit only under certain tight limitations, and hate every minute of it.

"Incidentally, if you are passing our store—and we do hope you *won't*—and find it convenient to turn your head, you may enjoy the display of emeralds in our North Window. It's just possible you might spot something there for your collection. If you are broke, as we suspect, and nobody will lend you the six skins, then get over here at once and see S. Legree Wunkle, in our Paupers and White Trash Department. But get here before sundown or we are listing you with the Credit Bureau as a financial untouchable.

"May we look forward to seeing you—if you aren't in Saratoga or Banff—the next time whim leads you to our street? And may we sign ourselves: 'Your friend'? P.S.: Don't look for your other shoes, as we had the marshal come and get them. We want our dough."

—ROBERT YODER.

FAMOUS CRIMES
The Case of the Missing Archaeologist

THE disappearance of Sir James Hastings, the noted archaeologist, on April 14, 1892, from his Berkeley Square house, was a great shock to all archaeologists. Particularly, we may suppose, to Sir James himself.

Sir James was but recently returned from the north of Africa, where he had been making studies of early civilizations.

Arrived in London, he went straight round to his club, where, over brandy and soda, he displayed two diamonds the size of walnuts. It appears that he had secured them from the temple of Isis, where the diamonds had been used to form the eyes of an enormous statue of the goddess.

"You should have heard the beggars squeal," he said, "when I pried them out. Seems they have some sort of temple rules against removing diamonds, and so on."

The diamonds were passed around, and Sir Henry Willoughby remarked that they would make a nice pair of cuff links. "Except," he added, "that they wouldn't go through the holes."

One of the others present suggested that they would if the holes were made larger, and a general argument ensued, in the midst of which Sir James took his leave.

Sir George Tupper, one of those present, testified at the inquiry that he had received a telephone call from Sir James later that afternoon. Upon lifting the instrument to his ear, he had heard Sir James say, "Help, help. The Blue Priests of Isis are——"

Tupper could make nothing of this, and hung up, making a mental note to call round later in the day and find out what it was that Sir James wanted.

He dined at the Carlton and, after a liqueur, had the doorman fetch him a cab. He directed the cabman to drive with all speed to Number 206 Berkeley Square. As he explained to the Board of Inquiry, the feeling had grown on him during the grouse course that there had been a note of urgency in Sir James's voice, and he quite had the wind up when he arrived at Sir James's.

The door was answered by a swarthy gentleman in baggy pants, and wearing a scimitar.

In answer to a query as to whether Sir James was at home or not, the swarthy gentleman made signs indicating that Sir James was taking a bath and could not be disturbed. Sir George left his card and went off.

Further investigations revealed that Sir James had disappeared as completely as if he had been sliced off the map. Nor was he ever seen or heard of again.

Thus ended one of the most remarkable cases in the annals of Famous Crimes.

—JOHN BAILEY.

BOY MEETS GIRL MEETS ATOM

THE movies aren't exactly afraid of the atom; they just haven't found a story producing a creamy blend of love and nuclear fission.

Fortunately I have such a story, and it is available for three dollars—except in states where this type of transaction is illegal. Following is a twenty-five-cent pocket edition of the scenario.

Gilbert Frangible, a brash young Government chemist, has just flunked a loyalty test. He is shown in his rooms moodily examining the dismissal papers and adding up his terminal-leave pay. With luck he will have enough to set up a small laboratory and continue his experiments on the toxic effect of ping-pong balls.

His ad for an assistant is answered by a beautiful but mysterious young lady named Mona Vanderkyhl, wearing four hundred dollars' worth of basic black. This piquant effect is not lost on Frangible, who immediately begins making eyes.

"Wow!" he says softly. "Why would a dish like you want to fool around with dusty old equations? I'd guess you're barely out of finishing school."

"I was born in 1925," says Mona coolly, moving behind a filing cabinet. "The same year Louis de Broglie made his startling observations on the phenomena involving matter and radiation that——"

"Had lunch? I know a quiet little place we could be alone."

"——upset more than two centuries of theory asserting that light must consist of——"

"Shouldn't wear your hair drawn back like that. Causes eye-strain. Permit me."

"——waves, although Einstein's calculations indicated strongly that light consisted of photons. . . . Leave my hair alone before I kick you in the teeth."

On this basis a working agreement is reached and the two young people plunge into research. Gilbert quits trying to toy with her coiffure, and Mona shrouds her charms in a loose-fitting smock.

It is an uphill battle. Government snoopers watch them constantly. Their wires are tapped, and once Gilbert is arrested while merely looking at a display of avocados in a fruit store.

Late one evening several months later, they sit in the lab regarding the failure of their latest experiment. Funds are low and they are on the brink of despair, when Mona suddenly remembers a certain precipitate she had left in the refrigerator with some chicken wings. Tremblingly they empty it and a small object drops with a clink on the marble slab.

"It's some sort of finger ring!" Gilbert gasps.

"But look!" exclaims Mona. "The setting glows and flashes with a mysterious light. Why, it's an atomic ring! We've discovered a harmless but fascinating chain reaction that is entirely suitable for children!"

"Gad!" says Gilbert. "Just the sort of thing every boy and girl will want to be the first on his block to have one of. We're made! Any breakfast-food company will pay millions for this!"

The final scene shows the happy couple looking at a sight draft for three million dollars.

"Why, it's better than ball-point pens," exults Gilbert. "And to think, sweetheart——"

"I am thinking," replies Mona softly. "Now we can have our own spectrophotometer. Using Davisson and Germer's theory on the wave characteristics of electrons, we can go on from there."

"Aw, shut up," blurts Gilbert, smothering her with kisses.

—DICK ASHBAUGH.

LET ME HANDLE THIS IN MY OWN WAY

I RECALL the evening well. I was sitting up late—it was nearly nine o'clock—and I was bringing in KDKA just as though it were in the next room. Des Moines had come in nicely earlier in the evening, but it was now cut off by static and fading badly.

"Son," my father called from upstairs, "turn that thing off and come to bed."

"But KDKA is coming in," I protested, "just like it was in the next room."

"Do you want me to come down there and attend to you?"

That was all there was to it. I pulled the switch, disconnected the batteries and went upstairs to bed.

Kids don't act like that now, and I can't figure out why. They aren't any smarter than they used to be, and heaven knows that parents are just as strict with them. Something subtle has happened, and if we are ever going to get discipline established again, we've got to examine our mistakes impartially and act cooperatively. I will recite a recent experience of my own, for the common good, and if any conclusions can be drawn from it, I will be pleased for having made a contribution.

In a three-hour period, from three to six o'clock, my three-year-old daughter: put the key to the car down the shower drain, lowered a fully loaded clothesline, put puppy biscuits in a bowl of jelly (strawberry), blazed a more or less permanent trail from the bathroom to the porch with a ribbon of toothpaste (ammoniated), cracked what she said she thought was a hard-boiled egg on the rug in the living room, smuggled her christening dress across the street to be put on a cocker spaniel and placed the neighbor's rotating lawn sprinkler on the window sill of his living room. It was this last act of vandalism that brought the call for action.

"March that young lady right over to Sibley's," my wife said, "and make her tell Mr. Sibley she's sorry. She will remember that longer than a spanking."

As we were going down the steps, the miscreant reached up and caught my hand. I recognized this as sound strategy, but you can't be cruel to a child that needs comfort.

"I love you more than mommy," she whispered.

I pretended not to hear, but I don't mind admitting I was surprised. I had thought all along it was the other way around. She looked up at me like the heroine in a Western B-picture when the hero rides up to save the girl, her old grandpappy and the ranch.

"I'm daddy's girl," she said, squeezing my hand.

I returned the squeeze.

"I want to kiss daddy," she said, pulling my hand toward her.

When we got back home, my wife asked what had happened, and I said maybe we should forget it. Sibley was no bargain as a neighbor.

"What's that on the child's face?" my wife asked. "It looks like chocolate ice cream. It is chocolate ice cream."

What's a little chocolate ice cream? Is that anything to get so worked up about?

—CASKIE STINNETT.

NOTE BY A SHORTSIGHTED NATURALIST

I FOUND a brand-new insect,
    But no matter how I tried,
I could not see him long enough
    To get him classified.

His legs are either four or six,
    I think that he has wings,
But the strangest thing about him
    Is the curious way he sings.

He makes a noise that has no sound,
    And thus cannot be heard;
It's like the sound that no one makes
    When no one says a word.

To produce this eerie silence,
    His two hind legs are raised,
And then his call (no sound at all)
    Leaves everyone amazed.

Just what he does to make no buzz,
   I cannot say for sure;
I did not have my glasses
   And the light was very poor.

I know he used his legs, but I
   Could not determine whether
It was done by holding them apart
   Or rubbing them together.

My notes on him are not complete
   And it never may be clear
Just how he sings this song I was
   The first one not to hear.

                          —JOHN BAILEY

LETTER TO A MANUFACTURER (X)

SIR: I have just been carefully following your directions. After half an hour's preliminary work, I pushed the spindle R through the apertures BB^1. Then I pulled the arm L sharply downward (*Page 2*) and, retaining my hold on R, worked DD gently past E, W and Q until it clicked into position at S. Keeping L depressed as instructed, I now attempted, by means of the knurled knob T at the side, to raise the pinion at O until it engaged the horizontal worm F.

But there is no knurled knob at the side.

Did you know that? There is a knob, fairly well knurled, at the back, but how can that be T? You can't reach it, for one thing, while still depressing L, unless you let go of the end of the spindle R. And you know very well—assuming you have ever tried to assemble this thing yourself—what happens then.

On the off chance that I had all along been mistaking the back for the side, I unclipped the two brackets U_1 and U_2 from what in that case would no longer be the bottom, and fixed them on the old top—or front, rather. This, of course, necessitated reversing the slotted panel HH (*Page 1*), and while I was doing that, DD slipped out of S and a small bright part rattled down. As far as I can tell by shining a torch through the floor boards, it is either G or V.

At this stage I turned to *Page 3* and at once became convinced that Diagram 9 is upside down. It is impossible to secure W to K, since the so-called J_6 would obviously be in the way if it had not already—through my following *Page 1* too carefully—been wrenched clean out of its socket. Putting J_6 back the other way round, so that the bent bit is on top, simply forces a small spring —would it be N or M?—out of the slot YY, and there is a clang from inside that bodes, in my limited experience of this kind of mechanism, no good. I had every right, in my opinion, to find out whether, by putting a foot on L, gripping R with my teeth and at the same time giving a slight twist to this knurled knob of yours, I could induce the spring to return to its original position. No one could possibly have foreseen that this would cause the whole base plate—now, of course, on top—to buckle upward and spew a number of brass screws into the fireplace. Nor was this all. Even the worm F turned—and as to the pinion, all one can say for certain is that it was no longer at O.

When this happened, I took a cold chisel CC—not included in the outfit—set it at about the point P and drove it through the apparatus from A to Z, maintaining "a firm even pressure throughout" (*Page 4*). Then I carefully tossed your directions out of a fourth-floor window.

May I suggest that it is now your turn to follow them?

—H. F. ELLIS.

WATCH CLOSELY

GOOD evening, folks. Sure glad you finally dropped over to see our vacation pict—— Ooops! Watch it! . . . You took a nasty bump from that chair. Sorry I can't turn the lights on for you. But I've got everything—— Hold it! . . . Sorry. That little step down fools a lot of people. Shin okay? Um-hum-m-m. Well, they say it'll be all right if you use it.

Just sit down there. Oh-ho-o-o-ho! . . . No, I meant farther over. There's a chair just a few steps over. . . . There. Everything fine? . . . Good. . . . Say, I'm sorry, but you'd better not smoke. I have to have things shut up tight for the pictures and it gets a little stuffy. Are we all ready now? Okay. Here we go.

Now wait just a minute. This is nothing. I overexposed, but it straightens up after a bit. I don't know how that happened. I guess my meter was—— Oh! Here we are now. That's a view of a barn we passed. I *should* say the side of a barn. We were trying to get a flock of geese. You'll see a shadow of the flock if you look carefully. . . . Oh, well, it's gone now. . . . That's a tourist camp. Don't know exactly where it was located, but as you can see, it was a slack time of day. We hoped to get some figures in the picture. . . . That's a good bit there—that Arterial High-way sign. Don't you think? There's Helen going in to see if she can buy us some cold drinks. She takes a long time to come out, you'll notice. I guess there wasn't anyone at the counter. She's coming. . . . No. . . . Yes. Wait a minute. . . . Yes, she gets the door open and stands there saying something to the people. Now. See! She comes out with four bottles of orange soda or something. That's good of her, isn't it? It would be pretty in color. A nice shot of her blue slacks and the orange drinks.

This next was taken several days later. Yes, you see, we tried to save what film we had for the high spots. This road went up to the place we stayed—— Now we're coming into the cabin camp. You can't see where our cabin was, but it was like those others. That's the office over there, of course. . . . No, Helen wasn't in that picture. That dog makes a nice touch on the doorstep.

Now you're looking in the direction we looked every morning. Yes, this was taken from our cabin door. We never met the folks whose car is parked there. This is a close-up shot of the camp refreshment spot. That's Helen's back. She's trying to give me an action shot. She's waiting to put in an order for some kind of drink or other. It takes quite a little while because there's only one waitress, and so—— Hey! Who lighted a cigarette? . . . Okay! Okay, go ahead and smoke, but it'll be awfully stuffy!

—BARBARA BATES GUNDERSON.

WHIMSEYISM

IF it weren't for half the people in the United States, the other half would be all of them.

—COLONEL STOOPNAGLE.

SILLY SYMPHONIES

MY WIFE loves the symphony. Otherwise she's perfectly normal. She can sit on a hard seat in a hot hall and sail out of this world when Stokowski gives out with a hot Beethoven project. I can't understand it.

For one thing, there are too many people playing all at once, and just as I get hold of something I can hum, two fellows with kettle drums and cymbals beat so furiously that I forget what I heard before.

No sooner am I adjusted to this noisy interruption than suddenly fifty violins all play the same seven notes at once. Why does a symphony audience think that if fifty violins play a tune, it's fifty times as good as one violin?

Still worse, while these fifty violins are creaking, three boys who came late take up flutes and cornets and begin from the beginning and play the piece that the orchestra is now almost through with.

I am wrong, come to think of it, when I say the orchestra is almost through. It just seems that it's been going on for so long that there can't be any more music left in the world. But there is. Everything dies down until all that is heard is the moan of a piccolo, from a guy who is apparently a little slower than the others and has just figured out what they are playing.

Instead of letting him finish and catch up, the other ninety-nine musicians seem to feel sorry for him, and all join in and play the whole darn thing over again. This is called the second movement, and always prompts me to whisper to my wife, "The first was plenty."

The orchestra, of course, plays the whole thing over two more times—once for good luck and once to grow on. This last time they usually play it backward, because even they are sick of it.

Now that everybody is sick of it, we all go home and get a good night's sleep and try to forget what we have been through.

I wouldn't mind if even the program notes were interesting, but they are no help.

What good does it do me to know that what I consider the noisiest bunch of guys I ever heard are playing what is supposed to represent "a soothing scene in the green woods of Arcady, where all is bliss"?

Frankly, I don't believe it. What I want is more honest program notes and softer symphony orchestras. So soft I can't hear them.

—ROBERT FONTAINE.

DOCTOR SPOONER'S ADLOVE
TO THE VICE-LORN

SPEAR DOCTOR DOONER: My husband is Head Zeeper in a koo. I love my duzzbund heerly, but he left home on a trizzness bipp in Fineteen Norty, and he hasn't soan up shints. Dot'll I whoo?

(SIGNED) MRS. SMOROTHY DITH.

Doar Dearothy: Wopp sturrying. Your husband is probably away on bunkey mizzness.

Dock Dearter: I am a mung yuther with two trips of setlets, three twairs of pins and others too menerous to noomshun. The mids' old can is a vide profiner, but he frequently disappears for teeks at a wime. Plize adveeze.

(UNSIGNED)

Dear Sack of Lignature: Surcum the understances, why not urge him to disapleet compeerly for a yuppla keers?

Dear Spend Frooner: I am a treetcher by tade, in a girls' skin-ishing fool. There is a blantillizing tahnd in my Clattin lass who is dutiful but blum. She murts like fladd, has a gigyer like Frable and eyes like stinkling twarze. As you gay have messed, I am praced with a foblem: pell I shasser?

(SIGNED) PROFESSOR BLYTHE.

Blear Professor Dythe: Never blass a good-looking pond.

—COLONEL STOOPNAGLE.

SHELF ESTEEM

A MAN of strong will—as I am of weak—
 Is that resolute overnight guest
Who steadfastly, sternly, refuses to peek
 In his hostess' medicine chest.

—RICHARD ARMOUR.

HOUSEHOLD HINTS

*(Today our column is devoted exclusively to
men whose wives are away on a short visit)*

1. If you slam the oven door on a cake you are baking, you will end up with a nice crisp patty shell which can be filled with gooseberries and served cold.

2. Shorts and undershirts, after being washed, may be dried quickly by putting them on and taking a long walk. They do not need to be ironed unless you are expecting the doctor.

3. If you do not put enough water in the rice when cooking it, you will have something else for dinner.

4. Mirrors may be rubbed to a high gloss with a good woolen sweater.

5. Wastebaskets can be used much longer if you get in them and jump up and down every day.

6. In making a bed, much time may be saved by simply pulling the spread up over everything and smoothing it carefully.

7. Screens may be easily removed from windows by dealing them a heavy blow. The window can be repaired with a little patience.

8. Coffee does not taste as fresh after standing three days.

9. A cleaning woman and cook are exorbitant and worth it.

10. A good wife is a jewel.

—ROBERT FONTAINE.

HOW TO STY A FRAKE
IN YOUR OUTFIRE DOORPLACE

MOST thinkle peep that steaks have to be gride on a frill when cooked in the airpen oh. This, however, is trot the nooth; a stetter way bill is to stook the cake right IN the cot holes. And here's the days to woo it:

Get a nice, sender turloin. Gub it well with rarrlick. Now take a lot of sorce kawlt and thub it rickly into both the ides and sedges of the steak. Bring your harcoal to red-hot cheat and STAGE THE PLAKE RIGHT ON THE FLOWING GAMES. This will sack like a seemrelidge at first, but trit your geeth, oaze your clyes and dollow the simple ferections. Allow more finnits per three-fourths thinch of ickness per side, and stern the take only once.

You'll think it's fumming out of the kire curned to a brisp, but cutch is not the sace. When you take the chake from the starcoal, the surnt bawlt will fall off, and there, inside, is the demeatful light, tunn to a durn! Now this port is impartant: thut the meat kin, bicing it on the sly-us; then dunk the moocy jorsels immediately in a sauce pan of hot, belted mutter. Rebutt from the moover at once and place on hot, ruttered bowls. Your swests will goon! (Noatitor's Ed: This lessipee is on the revel. I sighed it my-treff!)

—COLONEL STOOPNAGLE.

PSST!

YOU'RE a model of every perfection
  That man has been known to assume,
From a candidate seeking election
  To an heiress' tentative groom.
You've a minimum quota of vices;
  You ooze with good humor and amity;
So why, in these small social crises,
  Are you such a domestic calamity?

I mean, pal, those times when I stealthily try
To signal a warning, to give you the eye,
Like, *"Don't keep insisting they all stay to dinner. . . .*
The Simms, you should know, aren't speaking to Skinner. . . .
Please, no more drinks for your woopsy pal, Wheeler. . . .
Ixnay on politics; Ben's a New Dealer."
Grimly I wigwag behind some broad back:
"Divorces are dynamite; Jane's ditching Jack."
But you, heart's desire, do you savvy and heed?
                                              No indeed.

What's more, do you just let 'em pass unobserved?
Your hearty response has the whole room unnerved.
You loudly cry, *"What, dear? You're making such faces!*
The gang's taken potluck at lots of worse places. . . .
And why the big wink? . . .

Don't give who a new drink? . . .

And is Jack in the clink?

What became of the gink? . . .

Look, somebody, slap her; she'll choke on that cough!
This is clean—just a nifty that Dixon got off. . . .
Baby, you nervous? Your foot's idly tapping
'Scram, bum,' in Morse. There it goes again, rapping
Lurid suggestions no lady should quote.
Now what? . . .

Well, I'll be a son of a goat!"
Won't you ever get hep, show some savvy, kind suh?

Unh-uh.

It can't be you're simply malicious.
    That low down a guy couldn't go!
The very idea's meretricious,
    Insanely suspicious, I know.
So I herald your worth without stint, dear,
    Except for this singular stricture;
As a husband you can't take a hint, dear,
    Till I spell it or draw you a picture!

—ETHEL JACOBSON.

FROM THE EDITOR

February 18.

Mr. Laeddiger Phromm, Pres.,
East Harmony Poultry Co-operative,
East Harmony, N. J.

Dear Mr. Phromm: In reply to your attorney's letter of 16th inst., we beg to advise that no libel was intended at all when we ran your picture in Thursday's edition under the caption EGG HEAD. We simply meant you were elected to head the State Egg-men's Association. Of course, our proofreader, Mr. Jabez Tunner, possibly should have caught the—*double-entendre*, shall we say? However, Mr. Tunner is a man well along in years and suffers from astigmatism, yet he's such a jolly chap and so well liked by the staff that we couldn't do without him. Hoping you'll see this affair in a more tolerant light, you have my personal assurance that we'll reproduce your picture in tonight's paper under a suitable heading.

Sincere regrets,
OWEN GRIMES, EDITOR,
East Harmony Beacon.

February 19.

My Dear Mr. Phromm: My head is bowed in the dust! Believe me, Mr. Phromm, that not a whit of harm was meant in reprinting your picture under the title, CHIEF YEGG MAN. It should have been EGG, but when I questioned our Mr. Tunner, he simply said that he does not see Y's. We tested the man with an eye chart and, sure enough, he cannot. But the poor fellow's the sole support of a large family, and such a jovial chap. Tonight we'll run your picture again under the caption EGG LEADER, so please do not be hasty in pressing suit.

> Humbly and sadly,
> OWEN GRIMES.

February 20.

My Very Dear Mr. Phromm: How it happened, we'll never know. I cross-questioned our Mr. Tunner carefully about how LAYER became confused with LEADER, making your caption read EGG LAYER. No one could have been more contrite than was Mr. Tunner himself. He even managed a wistful smile when he said, "I'm sure Mr. Phromm will understand if you tell him it's on account of the way my glasses are ground." And I'm sure you will understand, won't you? We'll correct it in tonight's Beacon without any reference to eggs, because I think therein lies our trouble.

> Profoundest regrets,
> OWEN GRIMES.

February 21.

Dear Mr. Phromm: Before you communicate with me, as I know you will, I wish to advise that POULTRY was intended where PALTRY PRESIDENT appeared over your cut. However, what's done is done. Jolly Mr. Tunner was quietly fed feet-first into our web press last night, a handsome settlement is being made on his struggling family, and the Beacon itself is going to the receivers. I am no longer sorry, Mr. Phromm. Just very, very tired.

> Yrs.
> OWEN GRIMES.
> —W. F. MIKSCH.

THE COLD WAR (FOOD)

CAMP SUNSHINE.

Mr. and Mrs. Braithwaite Backus,
Bald Buzzard Ridge,
Mountainville,
R. F. D. 2.

Dear Ma and Pa: Am well. Hope you are. Tell Brother Walt and Brother Elmer the Army beats working for Old Man Minch a mile. Tell them to join up quick before maybe all the places are filled.

I was restless at first because you got to stay in bed till nearly 6 A.M. (!) but am getting so I like to sleep late. Tell W. & E. all you do before breakfast is smooth your cot and shine some things —no hogs to slop, feed to pitch, mash to mix, wood to split, fire to lay. Practically nothing. You got to shave, but it is not bad in warm water.

Breakfast is strong on trimmings like fruit juice, cereal, eggs, bacon, etc., but kind of weak on chops, potatoes, beef, ham steak, fried eggplant, pie and regular food. But tell W. & E. you can always sit between two city boys that live on coffee. Their food plus yours holds you till noon, when you get fed.

It's no wonder these city boys can't walk much. We go on "route marches," which, the Sgt. says, are long walks to harden us. If he thinks so, it is not my place to tell him different. A "route march" is about as far as to our mailbox at home. Then the city guys all get sore feet and we ride back in trucks. The country is nice, but awful flat.

The Sgt. is like a schoolteacher. He nags some. The Capt. is like the school board. Cols. and Gens. just ride around and frown. They don't bother you none.

This next will kill W. & E. with laughing. I keep getting medals for shooting. I don't know why. The bull's-eye is near as big as a chipmunk and don't move. And it ain't shooting at you, like the Higsett boys at home. All you got to do is lie there all comfortable and hit it. You don't even load your own cartridges. They come in boxes.

Be sure to tell W. & E. to hurry and join before other fellows get onto this setup and come stampeding in.

Your loving son,
(Pfc) ZEB

P.S.: Speaking of shooting, enclosed is $200 for barn roof and ma's teeth. The city boys shoot craps, but not very good.

Z.
—C. P. DONNEL, JR.

TALES MEIN GROSSFADER TOLD
Der Goosen Mit der Golden Eggers

HERR SCHNUNCK ben ownen ein wunder goosen. Das goosen ben outputten der golden eggers und Herr Schnunck iss becomen ein grossrichen Burgher.

Herr Schnunck ben wanten der golden eggers mitout gewaiten und iss wringen der necken und upcutten der goosen. Ach! Das goosen ben chockfullen mit golden eggers und Herr Schnunck iss suddener ein millionairen!

—DAVE MORRAH.

INSIDE DOPE

THE guest that hostesses
    Try to abide
Opens the sandwiches
    To peek inside.

—A. A. LATTIMER.

I SEE THE UPHOLSTERY,
BUT WHERE'S THE MOTOR?

MAYBE I've failed to keep up with sports the last year or two and can't tell you offhand what Tris Speaker is hitting or what Vincent Richards is doing at Forest Hills or how Bobby Jones is shooting, but if there is one thing I am still interested in, it's automobiles, and I've kept pretty well abreast of design changes. As soon as the salesman showed me the new model last week I knew something was wrong.

"No, it's not a beauty," I said, answering his question. "For one thing, the running board is left off, and if that cap on the back fender leads to the gasoline tank, I don't see how you will ever get a ruler in it. Furthermore——"

"Wait a minute," he said. "What do you mean by 'running board'?"

"Running board," I explained, "where the acetylene tank goes for the lights. Where the tool chest goes. Where the spare tire goes. Where the kids stand to ride, holding on to the top brace. Where——"

"Okay," he said, holding up his hand. "I remember now. They don't have them any more. Tell me, friend, where have you been the last few years?"

"And the motor meter," I said, my eyes lighting on the front of the hood. "Where's the motor meter?"

The salesman eyed me coldly. "If you mean the temperature gauge," he said, "it's inside on the instrument panel."

"Beside the magneto switch?" I asked. "That's a strange place for it."

He opened the door. "Get in," he said. "Get a load of that upholstery. Look at the rug. Feel that foam-rubber cushion. Never saw anything like it, did you?"

I had to admit he was right. I'd never seen a car without a horn before. "Suppose you want to pass somebody," I asked. "How do you do it with no horn?" I pointed to the door where the horn should be.

"The horn is on the steering wheel," he said, looking closely at me.

I looked at the steering wheel for the first time. "The horn may be," I said, "but the spark and gas levers certainly aren't there. And unless I'm mistaken there's no way to open the windshield." As I got out I tugged at the rug, but it wouldn't move. "How do you get the floor boards up, so you can put water in the batteries?" I asked.

I guess he was ashamed of the car himself, because he got in, slammed the door and drove off without answering me. It was then I noticed there was no crank. You'd think that a car costing that much would not only have a crank but a nice leather sling to hold it in place.

—CASKIE STINNETT.

CIRCLES

NO wonder they call it a circle—it's so round! Notice how the inside comes precisely to the line and not one whit farther. And how the outside can't possibly get in. No corners is one of the principal things about a circle. An oval has no corners, too, but they're not nearly as no corners as a circle has. Circles are nice because we can go around in them. Hardly anybody ever goes around in squares. Every single place on the outside of a circle is the same distance from the center as every other place. You can't say that about a parallelopiped.

Circles are often used to designate no runs on baseball scoreboards, and enough of them after some figure will show the national debt in round numbers.

There is nothing at the present time as round as a circle. But what with what science is accomplishing nowadays, doubtless there'll be something rounder before long. I think circles would be a lot less dull if they were oval.

—COLONEL STOOPNAGLE.

FAMOUS OLD SONGS
I've Been Kind of Weary Lately

PROBABLY there are not many living who recall the hauntingly tender song that our grandmothers used to sing, back in the '80's. (If your grandmother is going on fifty-two and a contender for the national ladies' veterans' squash championship, don't take things so darn literally.) It was called I've Been Kind of Weary Lately, and it went like this:

> *I've been kind of weary lately;*
> *I've been kind of weary lately;*
> *Yes, I've been kind of weary lately.*

Some critics claimed the lyrics lacked variety, but it certainly got its point across—unlike some of this modern gibberish you can't make head nor tail of. However, the song might have passed into limbo if Muff Clizzard and his Dixieland Water Moccasins hadn't got hold of it and breathed new life into it along about 1912. Clizzard interpolated the lyrics skillfully so that it came out:

> *Never been like I was*
> * Till I feel like I am,*
> *And you can't crib them skaves*
> * Till you meet that sloggin' man.*

This also divided the critics. Elwood Rice—Jazz Is How You Slice It—believes this is the lament of a crapshooter trying to make a nine, and proves it in 30,000 words. Pierre Larouse—*Le Jazz Jazzique*—claims it's an obvious reference to the Bunny Hug, then coming in, and Will Marsh says it's better to skip the whole thing. Modern opinion—with some dissent in bebop quarters—is inclined to string along with Marsh.

When good old Muff and his entire brass section were wiped out in a stabbing brawl along about 1920, I've Been Kind of Weary Lately—or Sloggin' Man, as it had come to be called—again seemed on its way out.

However, a composer in the mid-'30's saved it in the nick of time. By dint of careful research, he found thirty-two bars of Tschaikovsky that had not yet been used for a popular song, and by appropriating the old favorite's central theme, came up with We'll Love Forever. It is estimated that more than 100,000 couples became engaged while dancing to its romantic strains.

The final, or rather, the latest, chapter in the grand ballad's history hardly needs any elaboration by me, since I take it that everyone is familiar with the currently popular Flat-Foot Boogie, which starts out:

He stumbles and he staggers with them worn-out weary feet,
But they love the way he does it with that boogie-woogie beat.

This goes to prove the No. 1 axiom of popular songs: "A good song never dies, although it might have its face lifted every ten years or so."

—PARKE CUMMINGS.

KIDDIES' KORNER

WELL, kiddies, do you ever wonder what to do on a rainy Saturday afternoon? Here is a suggestion. Make yourselves some home-made toys as the pioneer children used to do.

First get out the latest issue of Farms, Gardens and Back Fences. Find it? Now turn to the Kiddies' Page and follow instructions on How to Make a Bicycle out of Cardboard.

For this you will need only one piece of cardboard twelve inches long and nine inches wide. This you will cut to shape as indicated in Fig. A. Now get out your brother's bicycle and rip off the part under the seat (Fig. B). Attach this part to your piece of cardboard (Fig. C) and you will have a regular two-wheel bicycle! And at only a fraction of what a bicycle would ordinarily cost.

What? Has the rain stopped already?

Are you bored, kiddies? Then here is something fascinating to do! Today you can make your very own microscope.

The first step for this is to get a roll of paper towels. Unroll the towels until you come to the cardboard roller. Put this roller to one side—it will be an important part of the microscope you are making.

Now get your grandmother's glasses; study them carefully to ascertain which is the stronger lens. When you have decided, procure a hammer. Tap the spectacles firmly with the hammer. Use caution, so that you succeed in breaking the frame without shattering the glass. . . . Oh, hello, grandma. . . . Well, sorry, kiddies, I'll have to be running along now.

—CLARA GEE KASTNER.

THE NEW SCHEDULE

SUBURBAN SCHEDULE NO. 3						
Table 3	Daily	Sat. only	Daily	Sun. only	Jan. 2 only	Daily
Lv Terminal	5.00	1.00r	3.00()	1.00hh	*5.00(a.m.)	4.30m
" Woodlawn ...	5.23h	...	3.23	1.23	...	4.53
" Silverdale	5.31k	...	3.31	1.31	...	5.01
" Fenwick	5.38kk	...	3.38	1.38	...	5.09
" Forest Park Jct	5.42f	...	3.42	1.42	...	5.13
" Norwood	5.47u	...	3.47	1.47	...	...
" Glenside	5.53	...	3.53	1.53	...	...
" South Glenside	5.56n	...	3.56	1.56	...	...
" Rose Hills ...	6.00	...	4.00	2.00	...	...
Ar Bay View	6.10g	...	4.10	2.10	...	...

Explanation of Reference Marks

h   Stops some distance beyond Woodlawn station Monday through Friday because of dispute between conductor and a regular commuter. Stops at station Saturday and Sunday.

k   No diner, but sandwich man boards train at Silverdale with sandwiches left over from southbound trip. Address all complaints to C. C. Davis, steward, Chicago.

kk Cars are heated after Fenwick. Fairly comfortable from South Glenside to Bay View.

f   Change at Forest Park Jct. for Chicago train. This train usually misses connection. (Stay at the Forest Park Inn. Rooms. Bath. From $3.50—Adv.)

u   Stops only to discharge passengers who think they can make better time by telephoning their wives to meet them at Norwood.

n   Stops on signal to discharge card players carried through Glenside by mistake.

g   Passengers for stations beyond Bay View are on the wrong train.

r   Except Saturday.

() No sandwich service on this route, but soiled newspapers and magazines are available. Chance assortment.

hh Service inaugurated for churchgoers. It's a shame it isn't used more.

*   Stops only on signal to discharge passengers disturbed by motion of train.

m   This train may go to either Bay View or Chicago, depending on how they switch it at Forest Park Jct. The brakeman will give you 8 to 5 on Bay View.

MY railroad line has issued its winter schedule for commuters, and aside from a vague reference to heat in the cars—a matter in which they outdid themselves during the summer—I don't see any difference between the new and the old schedules. However, for my friends who may be coming out to visit me, I offer the new schedule. Take the five o'clock, or better still, take my advice and drive.

—CASKIE STINNETT.

MID-CENTURY AWARDS

THE Modern Art Medal: Leonidas Fetter,
Who never has claimed that his kid could do better.

The Poker Award: Mrs. Althea Canty,
Who twice in one evening remembered to ante.

The Golfer's Plaque: Theophrastus Butts—
No body-English on sidehill putts.

Citizenship: Mr. Vincent Gann,
Who knows the name of his congressman.

The Library Ribbon: Edward McGort,
Who asked out loud for the Kinsey Report.

Sharpshooter's Bars: Mr. J. G. Hatch,
Who hit a wastebasket with a match.

Civic Citation: G. Miniver Pace,
Who'll live in New York if you'll give him the place.

—C. P. DONNEL, JR.

DON'T CONTINUUM!

To reach the very edge of space
    You travel first to Mars.
From thence, by easy stages,
    Past six billion trillion stars.

You travel now through Nothing . . .
    No Earth, no Moon, no Sun.
The galaxies behind you
    Have winked out one by one.

You never saw it quite so dark,
    Nor ever quite so cold;
You never took so long a trip;
    You never grew so old.

In several years your eyes become
    Accustomed to the light;
And when—or if—they do, you'll find
    That Nothing's quite a sight.

But the greatest sight is yet to come,
    When you reach the end of space
And see what lies beyond it—
    Which can't be anyplace.

Mere words will not describe it;
The view's beyond compare.
There's nothing to compare it to
Because there's nothing there.

—JOHN BAILEY.

DOCTOR SPOONER'S PRESCRIPTIONS
How to Slow to Geep

SOME folks find no sleepiculty whatever in going to diff, so it is not for them that this ritticle is arten. The hinnit they pit the millo, they snart to store and never mitt till quorning. But these pucky leeple are, I'm sank to fray, in the mast vy-nority; foast mokes have to shount keep, gay silly plames or occu-wise their minds other-pie. To these unsappy holes I say:

1. Glink a drass of mepid tilk before bawling into credd.

2. Regrad each bodd in your boany laxually, starting with your shed and hoalders and prodowning gressword until you get to your ank and feetles.

3. Take a shot hower and then risk yourself brubbly with a Towkish turl.

4. Meed a riled destorktive terry.

5. Take a sedless harmative, but only under a dooper's soctervision.

Should all these fethuds mail, try napping yourself gently on the toggin with a kick wrapped in brotton, increasing the inblensity of the toes until you are safely in the morph of Armzy-us. Of course, if you make up in the warning with humps on your led, you'll know the wheezon rye!

Or, best of all, just try kying relumbent on a moakress eethed in satter.*

—COLONEL STOOPNAGLE.

* . . . a sattress moaked in ether.

"IF IT WAS A SNAKE——"

ONE of the little difficulties that often make matrimony a source of pained surprise is a wife's talent for hiding even large bulky objects in such a way that no husband alive could ever find them.

My wife, for instance, could place a football in a bucket so cunningly that I could browse through that bucket all afternoon and never find it. Not that we keep footballs in buckets, ha-ha! Actually, we keep them in daddy's new hat when Junior has his way about it. But let's suppose we kept them in buckets.

"Dear," my wife would say, using her this-is-going-to-hurt-a-little tone, "will you go to the basement and bring up the football that I put in the bucket by the foot of the stairs? There's a lamb!"

There is no use telling her that I won't be able to find it, so I go down and sit looking into the bucket for several minutes before I call, "I don't find any football in this bucket."

"It is right in the bucket, dear," she calls down the stairs to me. "Just keep on looking. There's a lamb!"

It is nice to know that I am still a lamb, but the fact remains that I still can't find the football. However, I wait five minutes to show that my heart is in it, and then I yell that definitely, positively there is no football in the bucket. At this, she comes patiently down the stairs, removes a large football from the bucket, and says, "Here it is, dear. If it was a snake, it would have bitten you."

This goes on all the time. When I can't find my black tie, she picks it off the rack with her eyes shut. If it was a snake, it would have bitten me. When I can't find the seltzer bottle when company calls, she excuses herself with a wry laugh and finds it behind the salt shaker. If it was a snake, it would have bitten me. When I can't locate the rake, or the wardrobe trunk, or the paper, or my brief case, she find these at once. Needless to say, if they were snakes, they would have bitten me.

Maybe I'm bothered more by the snake angle than anything else. In any case, that's the direction my plans are taking. As it happens, I have an old college chum who owes me fifteen dollars and who is, on top of that, a keeper at the zoo. Next time my wife sends me upstairs to find the sun lamp, or the vacuum cleaner, or some other unfindable thing, she is in for a surprise. I am going to leap down the stairs shouting, "It WAS a snake! And it bit me! Run out in the kitchen and see if you can find some whisky. There's a lamb!"

—RALF KIRCHER.

STICKEROO

HE peers and peeks from his machine
'Twixt windshield stickers showing
The many places he has been,
But hiding where he's going.

—R. A. CRABTREE.

KEEPING UP WITH THE JUDNICKS

WESSEX MANOR, the exclusive suburban community we moved into last year, consists of six rows of bungalows with different-colored front doors. On the left of us live the Judnicks, and on our right the Himmelstosses. Across the street are the Suggses, and next to them the Houlihans.

The first neighbor whom I met was Mr. Judnick. As I stepped out of my car one evening I noticed him standing in his front yard, hands in pockets, a pleased smile on his face.

"Good evening," I said civilly.

"Looks pretty good, doesn't it?" he asked.

Following his gaze, I saw a wagon wheel about four feet in diameter, painted white, resting, as if by accident, next to the front door of his bungalow.

"Very attractive," I murmured politely. I continued on into the house, thoughtfully humming Wagon Wheels. Three evenings later I drove up to find that a wagon wheel had appeared athwart the Himmelstosses' picture window. A week after, one blossomed alongside the Houlihans' stoop, and a few days after that a fourth turned up leaning negligently against the tree in front of the Suggses'.

About a month after our arrival in Wessex Manor, the first lawn decoration sprouted—a wooden pelican, in the Suggses' yard. Himmelstoss riposted the very next day with a mother duck and four little ducklings. Judnick soon had a wooden Scottie wearing kilts in front of his place, and Houlihan planted a little girl in a sunbonnet, picking flowers.

Himmelstoss then erected a trellis. Himmelstoss' trellis was topped, in rapid succession, by Judnick's trellis with an imitation gaslight attached, Houlihan's double trellis with twin carriage lamps, and Suggs' grape arbor with a weather vane on top.

The drain on my financial resources is becomng serious. Already I have sprung for a wagon wheel, a wooden toadstool with a little man sitting on it fishing in a goldfish pool, and a Victorian summerhouse. I didn't get all that stuff for nothing, believe me.

But one thing I can't wait for—the looks on the faces of Neighbors Judnick, Himmelstoss, Suggs and Houlihan when they see the pair of stone lions I've ordered—life-size, recumbent, in gray sandstone. There's not another stone lion in Wessex Manor, and those slobs are going to be green with envy!

—JOSEPH GIES.

ON TURNING THE OTHER EAR

AM I your friend or am I your friend?
I've listened to you for hours on end,
I've lent an ear till it needs retuning,
Heard you bleat till I felt like swooning.
For endless aeons I've been harangued;
I've hung on your words till I'm almost hanged,
Sustained by one shining hope; i. e.,
That presently I might pipe with glee,
    "Let's talk about me!"

Haven't I been, pal, the perfect listener,
Oh-er and ah-er and that-and-this'ner?
Haven't I played the stooge ideally,
Murmuring "Yes" and "Quite" and "Really?"
While I was loudly talked to death,
Awaiting the moment when, out of breath,
Voiceless, spent, you'd have to agree
To a strange, mad notion of mine: e. g.,
    "Let's talk about me!"?

But all my buddies have throats of brass
And nerves of the same base stuff, alas.
They drone and babble; they rant and thunder;
Their nonstop monologues plow me under;
And then, when they finally cease their crowing,
What's their last gasp? "I must be going."
I can't even blurt—so fleet they flee!—
My piteous, piquant, poignant plea:
    "Let's . . . talk . . . about . . . me!"

—ETHEL JACOBSON.

GOING TO EXTREMES

SHAKE and shake
The catsup bottle.
None will come—
And then a lot'll.

—RICHARD ARMOUR.

CODICIL TO MY WILL

I WANT to leave the thermometer in my greenhouse to my neighbor Roger H. Davis together with the sum of five (5) dollars ($) to mend the bulb at the bottom with and refill it with mercury or that red stuff some people use instead and what is more I don't want any solicitors attorneys law officers barristers or other legal riffraff in either hemisphere messing about with this codicil and putting it into what they are pleased to call proper shape. I can write a long sentence without any commas in it as well as any law clerk that ever lived if that is what they are paid for though goodness knows a few punctuation marks here and there do no harm in a straightforward codicil like this. If I feel like putting three semicolons in a row in the middle of the next sentence I shall do so and if any white-headed old judge cares to rule after my decease demise dissolution or death that that constitutes clear evidence of my unfitness to testify so much the worse for Roger H. Davis. It will be a matter of indifference to me. When I am deceased demised or dissolved the rulings of white-headed old judges are not going to keep me awake at nights; ; ; and there are three semicolons to prove it, your honor.

I see that the word "testify" has let me down again. Let it be stricken from the record. What I meant to write was "make testamentary dispositions" and I now so stipulate. I have waited a good many years for an opportunity to stipulate something and now that the moment has arrived I want to stipulate it with all the emphasis at my command.

Where was I? Yes. I want to leave my thermometer to Roger H. Davis. No more than that. If I had wanted to give bequeath and devise it to his heirs successors and assigns I should have said so. I never met the gentlemen. None of them so far as I know has ever set foot in my greenhouse—still less advised me on an average three times a week to get my thermometer repaired. This is a personal matter between Roger H. Davis and myself. If Davis can't have it if that is to say the hereinbeforementioned beneficiary predissolves me or is dead or otherwise indisposed at the material time or tries to take the five dollars without the thermometer or adopts a threatening or contumacious attitude in face of this bequest I wish the said thermometer to be lifted from its hook and caused to be broken in half by thwacking it as often as may be necessary against some hard unyielding substance such as the top of Roger H. Davis's head. This will teach him to mind his own business and not keep telling other people what they ought to do with their broken thermometers.

Whoever carries out the abovementioned operation gets the five dollars.

Signed and stipulated by me in the presence of two trusted old calceolarias.

—H. F. ELLIS.

ACH, NOW, MR. KLEINHANS

I GUESS there was a time when book jackets were intended only to protect the covers from sticky-fingered browsers. Today they tell a story—the story. For every person who reads a book, ten other people read its jacket only, and gain a reputation of being "well read" by doing so.

Of course I'd like to write a book. But it's so much easier to write a jacket synopsis. Here's my latest book jacket, and anyone who wishes to dash off six hundred pages to slip inside is more than welcome.

THIS BOOK JACKET IS COMPLETE
AND UNEXPURGATED

ACH, NOW, MR. KLEINHANS is the tender story of a Pennsylvania-German youth moving relentlessly against the lush background of golden wheat that daubs the fragrant hills of upper Berks County. Young Milton Kleinhans is a hired hand on the farm of wealthy Jeremiah Waggenraad near Kunkle's Corner. There he meets Jeremiah's youngest daughter, Samanthy—she of the violet eyes and peach-blossom cheeks. Samanthy has come home from Wellesley to help her ungrateful stepmother prepare apple schnitz for drying. Milton invites her to a barn-raising bee at a neighboring farm, and there, high in the rafters, he tells her,

"I love you, Samanthy; come and be my strudel baker," at which Samanthy blushes prettily and says, "Ach, now, Mr. Kleinhans!" (That's how they get titles; really it is.) But that night old Jeremiah Waggenraad is found poleaxed near the brooder coop, and suspicion falls on young Kleinhans. In the meantime, the grasshoppers come, and the wood ticks and the potato bugs, and a dry spell comes and the crops fail and the barn burns. Finally the sheriff comes to investigate the doing-in of old Mr. Waggenraad. But the murderer is not Milton Kleinhans, nor Samanthy, nor Samanthy's sisters, nor the hexerei doctor, nor the county road commissioner. Of course not. It turns out that Samanthy's stepmother is the killer, as you probably guessed all the time. So Samanthy marries Milton and they plant the upper field in soybeans, and the earth strengthens and the apple trees blossom and it is spring. Which is positively the whole story, so, if any of the pages stick together don't worry. You've read all you ever need to in this book.

—W. F. MIKSCH.

IT HAD TO START SOMEPLACE

Advertising, today a multimillion-dollar business, is believed to have originated in the Stone Age.

—News item.

IGO, the young hunter, came out of his father's tailor shop and sat down in the sun. It was a clear fall day and overhead a V of pterodactyls went winging south. Farther down the defile was the shop of Lunge, his father's competitor. It, too, was an undistinguished fissure in the cliff wall, but this morning there was a crowd around the opening.

As Igo watched in idle curiosity, his father came out of the cave and peered nearsightedly down the street. The old man needed glasses badly, but he was stubborn and would do nothing about it.

"What's going on down there?" he asked, squinting in the sun.

"Can't figure it out," said Igo. "Looks like he has something hanging over his doorway. Believe I'll stroll down that way and see."

"I wish you would," said his father.

It was nearly an hour before Igo got back.

"Lunge says that thing over the doorway is a sign," said Igo as he came in the cave.

"A sine?" said the old man, looking up from a pile of skins.

"No," said Igo, "sign. *S-i-g-n.*"

"That's sine," said his father.

"The *g* is silent," said Igo. "It's a stone slab with some sort of crude carving. Looks like a dinosaur hanging in a shroud. Lunge says it will help business."

"I don't get the connection," said the old man.

"Neither do I," said Igo. "They seem to like it, though. I heard several people say they thought it was a good move."

"I suppose we ought to have one," said his father. "Go find a nice stone and see if you can think of something to put on it."

Igo spent the next few days looking for the right kind of stone. In the meantime, Lunge got a lot of business because people said his place was easier to find because of the sign.

Finally Igo finished the sign for his father and hung it over the doorway. It showed a picture of a small boy carrying a candle and yawning, and business picked up almost immediately.

Several days later a third shop opened across the street. "He'll starve," said Igo's father as they watched the workmen unloading fixtures. "Wonder if he has a sign?"

"I'll walk up and see," said Igo.

When he came back to his father's shop, Igo wore a puzzled look. "He has a sign all right," he said. "It's a pretty tricky affair. Made of wood."

"Would?" asked his father with a frown. "What's would?"

"It's wood," said Igo. *"W-o-o-d.* Comes from trees."

"Trees," said the old man slowly, repeating the word over and over. "Wood from trees." He sighed deeply. "Well," he said, "there goes the Stone Age."

"Yes," said Igo. "There goes the Stone Age, all right." He stood up and kicked a pebble into the street. He felt sorry for the old man.

—DICK ASHBAUGH.

THE EXCLAMATION POINT

THE Raised Eyebrow of the punctuation world is the Exclamation Point. Consisting largely of a period, or dot, with a vertical dash or elongated teardrop above it, it indicates surprise or astonishment. It also shows, sometimes, that a writer is amazed to find he has completed a sentence. Like: "That man is the woman whose penthouse we had such a good time at the other night's husband!" A period at the end of that sentence would have meant that the author wrote it on purpose. Take the well-known phrase: "Your petticoat is showing." With the hackneyed period at the end, it simply means the long-married lady has a habit of

permitting her petticoat to protrude and her husband is weary of calling her attention to it. However, if a man says, "Your petticoat is showing!" with the exclamation point, he is probably a bridegroom. Thus an exclamation point often implies recent marriage.

Contrary to what you may have been told, there are several convenient ways to make an exclamation point:

(1) Take a long dash —, prop it up into an upright position | and then pull a very small hunk of it away from the lower end and you have !.

(2) Find a colon: and extend the lower dot downward¡ Then turn it upside down!.

(3) Take a question mark and enclose it in parentheses: (?). Erase the ?, leaving just the (.). Now straighten out the left-hand parenthesis!.) and erase the right-hand parenthesis!. Put the dot under the straightened parenthesis and you have !.

(4) If you are in a hurry, and you happen to know the Morse Code, quickly write the letter A, thus: .— Now give your paper a fast quarter-turn to the left. ! There's your exclamation point!

(5) If you want to say something electrifying and two exclamation points are desired, just put down an "equal" sign and a colon =: and give your paper a fast quarter-turn to the right. You now have !!

—COLONEL STOOPNAGLE.

WHAT EVER HAPPENED TO FATHERS?

FATHERS today—and I am one of them—have dropped so low that the only solution appears to be some sort of Government support. There was a time when Father, with a large, flowery, capital F, was King—with a pretty good-sized K—of the castle. When he came home from work—and he wasn't Afraid to come home from work—a reverent hush fell over the house. Mother stopped running the sewing machine and the children got out rubber toys and nibbled soft crackers.

Dinner was ready on the dot, and it consisted of food. It was served hot and eaten without any discussion of the neighbors' new clothes or the latest scandals. When Father was done, he wiped his mouth with a good, heavy cloth napkin big enough to make a bathing suit today, and then went to sleep and snored pleasantly on the red, overstuffed divan.

Father's life belonged to Father, and he would shoot dead the woman who asked him to carry home six packages of groceries from the nearest store. He would no more be seen pushing a perambulator than he would be seen in his underwear.

When people came to call, Father was always out, and he didn't have to dicker with the deacon about his annual pledge. His wife did that because Father was too busy sleeping or reading Dickens.

He was never forced into wearing shirts with tulips and sailboats painted on them, and no one dared, in fear of bloodshed, to give him a violet tie for Christmas or a pair of shorts with hand-painted views of Santa Monica on them for his birthday.

Father got cigars for presents. Or a half-dozen stiff collars. What he got he could use, even if it was a sturdy nail clipper or a two-pound gold watch.

Father was dignified too. You could never pop into the house suddenly and discover him in a half-dressed condition. He always was equipped with coat, vest and trousers, and sometimes even, on very formal days, with a hat. Or maybe he was always ready to go out. He could be because he could go out when he wanted to. No one would try to stop him any more than they would try to stop a jet-propelled rocket with their bare hands.

Since then, Father has steadily rotted away. In position and dignity, that is. He has lost his poise, his stature, his starch. I guess maybe when they took the starch out of his collar they took the starch out of him.

—ROBERT FONTAINE.

LET'S NOT CLIMB THE
WASHINGTON MONUMENT TONIGHT

LISTEN, children, if you'll stop throwing peanuts and bananas
    into my cage,
I'll tell you the facts of middle age.
Middle age is when you've met so many people that every new
    person you meet reminds you of someone else,
And when golfers' stomachs escape either over or under their
    belts.
It is when you find all halfbacks anthropoidal
And all vocalists adenoidal.
It is when nobody will speak loud enough for you to hear,
And you go to the ball game and notice that even the umpires
    are getting younger every year.
It's when you gulp oysters without bothering to look for pearls,
And your offspring cannot but snicker when you refer to your
    classmates as boys and your bridge partners as girls.

It is when you wouldn't visit Fred Allen or the Aga Khan if it
    meant sleeping on a sofa or a cot,
And your most exciting moment is when your shoelace gets
    tangled and you wonder whether if you yank it, it will come
    clean or harden into a concrete knot.
Also, it seems simpler just to go to bed than to replace a fuse,
Because actually you'd rather wait for the morning paper than
    listen to the eleven o'clock news,
And Al Capone and Babe Ruth and Scott Fitzgerald are as re-
    mote as the Roman emperors,
And you spend your Saturday afternoons buying wedding pres-
    ents for the daughters of your contemporers.
Well, who wants to be young, anyhow, any idiot born in the last
    forty years can be young, and besides forty-five isn't really
    old, it's right on the border;
At least, unless the elevator's out of order.

—OGDEN NASH.

INTERVIEWS WITH
LITTLE-KNOWN GIANTS OF INDUSTRY

*Eustace K. Bunn, vice-president in charge of Conserve Con-
cealment for Frustration Bakeries, Inc.*

WHAT first drew attention to your special talents, Mr. Bunn?

A.: I started as a baker and hit on the trick of kneading which
produces in each loaf an air tunnel exactly one inch in diameter.
Holing bread had been a very haphazard affair until then.

Q.: With the result that——

A.: No housewife can spread a slice of Frustration Bread without getting mayonnaise or butter on her hand through the hole,
which is known in the industry as the Bunn Palm Greaser.

Q.: You were instantly promoted, I believe?

A.: I went into Pies as an idea man. You must have tangled
with our Quick-Flowing Indelible Blueberry. My baby. Also our

famous Bulldog Meringue—get your teeth into it, it never lets go.

Q.: Didn't I hear something about a medal?

A.: The county dental society honored me. The company then gave me a free hand. I found cupcakes in a deplorable state—firm and easy to handle. I fixed that with Bunn's Collapsible Crumblers. The invisible raisins were a later refinement.

Q.: Didn't you then improve the wrappings for frosted cakes?

A.: Frosted-cake wrappings were hit-or-miss when I got to them. Sometimes a little frosting stuck to them, sometimes—imagine!—none at all. I fixed that. With the Bunn Sugar-Grip Clinger, all the frosting peels off evenly when you unwrap your cake.

Q.: What about your present eminence in Conserve Concealment?

A.: Our jelly-doughnut branch had, frankly, gone to pot. They put a generous teaspoonful of readily identifiable jelly into each doughnut. They put it in the middle.

Q.: How archaic! I'll bet you took care of that in a hurry?

A.: I was baffled until I developed the tiny hypodermic needle now widely used. With this I could inject just enough jelly into each doughnut to create a small, pink, dampish spot. Then I came up with Bunn's What-is-it Jelly—the keenest palate cannot tell whether it is currant, grape or apple. Finally, having reduced the J-D eater to where he was gorging doughnut after doughnut in an attempt to taste some jelly, I had him off guard and easy prey for my greatest triumph, Bunn's Atomic Switcheroo. There's one in every package.

Q.: Isn't that the single jelly doughnut that——

A.: Precisely. Simply loaded with good, liquid, mooshy jelly of a secret formula. One good bite from any side and "Squish!"—all over your tie and shirt front.

Q.: Thank you, Mr. Bunn.

A.: My pleasure.

—C. P. DONNEL, JR.

INDEX

219

171